Pitch by Pitch!

Winning Mental Game Strategies for Young Baseball Players

DR. CURT ICKES

Pitch by Pitch!

Winning Mental Game Strategies for

Young Baseball Players

Copyright © 2024 by Dr. Curt Ickes

First Paperback Edition: 2024

IRC Holdings Ltd

Ashland, OH 44805

ISBN: 9798320261041

Published by KDP

Edited by: Olivia Fisher, Zechariah Van Farowe, Cynthia Hilston

Cover Design by: Michael Bird

Cover Illustration by: Russell Gunning

Interior illustrations by: Russell Gunning, Hannah Keough, Riley Bennett

Pitch by Pitch!

Winning Mental Game Strategies
for Young Baseball Players

This book teaches important mental game skills to young baseball players. These skills are valuable in other sports and in daily life as well. Young readers learn effective strategies to handle pressure, recover from mistakes, manage emotions, and boost confidence. These are all critical skills that help them perform at their best.

Dive into the engaging story of Jack, Matt, and the Oak Grove Owls as they bring these important lessons to life. Their story is very relatable, because they go through the same struggles and triumphs as most young baseball players. With its easy-to-read style and enjoyable review sections after each chapter, this book ensures all readers can grasp and remember key points.

Additionally, 'Pitch by Pitch!' features a special coaches' guide. This guide takes coaches through every chapter step by step. Coaches can use these chapter summaries, practice exercises, and group discussion questions to teach their team the mental game. Learning these skills as a team helps everyone learn quicker, "speak the same mental game language," and support each other's good habits.

I hope this book brings pleasure and knowledge, both of which will make playing the game of baseball much more enjoyable and fulfilling.

Dr. Curt Ickes

Table of Contents

1

Practice, Pressure, and Ice Cream

"Jack! Jack! Over here!" shouted a tall boy with sandy hair, messy from the wind. He waved excitedly from the freshly cut outfield grass.

Jack shielded his eyes from the bright sun, and his mouth stretched into a huge smile. "Be right there, Matt!" he called back. With a loud thud, the young third baseman dropped his heavy bag in the dugout. He dug through the bag, pushing past old game balls, a sliding mitt, and some empty candy wrappers before finally finding his dusty mitt. He was eager to join his new teammates.

Sunlight danced off the empty bleachers as Jack sprinted towards right field. His team, the Oak Grove Owls, were already warming up for practice, their laughter and chatter filling the air. Everyone was in good spirits after last night's big win.

Slowing down, Jack called to Matt, "Can you believe we beat the Falcons?" he panted, as he reached Matt, his teammate and new best friend.

"That was your best game ever, especially that game-winning slide!" Matt said, grinning. "You looked sweet diving into home!"

"Thanks! Your mental game tips helped a lot," Jack said, tapping his chest. "My heart was racing, but those deep breaths you taught me really calmed me down. Your pre-pitch routine with that focus point worked great. I saw the baseball all the way from the pitcher's hand to my bat!"

"Yeah, I could see your focus," Matt said, his eyes dancing with happiness. "It's cool knowing exactly what to do before each pitch instead of just nodding when people yell, 'Just relax!' and 'Be confident!'" As he spoke, he scooped up a baseball and sent it arcing high toward Jack.

Squinting against the bright sun, Jack raised his glove and caught the ball just in time. "I hope we can keep our streak going."

"Same here," Matt nodded. "But you know, it's about playing one pitch at a time. If we do that, we will win the inning and then win the game."

"Alright, team, bring it in!" Coach Wolf yelled from the dugout.

The Owls hustled off the field, kicking up small dust clouds as they ran toward the dugout. Jack found a spot on the bench between two of his teammates, Noah and Matt.

Coach Wolf looked at his team proudly. "Awesome job beating the Falcons. They're tough, but we showed them! We're 2-0 for the year, and I'm proud of you." Coach Wolf paused as the Owls' cheers ricocheted around the dugout. When the cheers died out, he continued, "But our first tournament is tomorrow. It'll be another big test for us."

Glancing at his clipboard, Coach Wolf's eyes widened. "First, we're up against the Lattasburg Lizards. You guys know about L-Burg. We played them a few times last year, and they beat us every time. But this is a new season. Let's be ready to play our best!"

At the mention of the Lattasburg Lizards, Jack's eyebrows shot up, and he glanced around to see his new teammates' reactions.

Noah leaned back and rolled his eyes. "We've got the Lizards in our first game? Not cool. Last year they beat us alright. I'd say they drilled us. Wouldn't you say so, Matt?"

Matt nodded, frowning as he looked at the ground. Jack bit his lip and fidgeted with his glove.

"Let's practice hard for this weekend," Coach Wolf said. "Infielders with me. Outfielders with Coach Miller!"

Jack rose from the bench and sprinted out to the field, still full of energy. Jack cracked a smile again as he fielded balls smoothly at third base. His throws hit Noah's glove at first base every time. But Noah seemed distracted, dropping easy throws and missing ground balls through his legs or off his glove.

"Come on, Noah! You can do better!" encouraged Coach Wolf, as another ball slipped past Noah's glove.

Jack's eyes narrowed, and he tilted his head. *What's up with Noah? He's usually one of our best players. Is he still worrying about the Lizards?*

The Owls worked hard, hustling, and making each swing count. In the outfield, Matt dashed for a fly ball before making a diving catch. JJ pounded fastballs into the strike zone, hitting Cooper's target every time. Jack, Drew, and Noah effortlessly turned a double play.

***

As the setting sun painted the sky orange and pink, practice ended. The boys caught their breath, their faces glistening with sweat.

"Great job today! Don't forget, be at the field by nine. I want us there an hour early to prepare," said Coach Wolf. "Get a good night's sleep and come ready to play!"

As Coach Wolf's voice faded, the boys, with shirts clinging to their sweaty backs, packed their gear, weighed down by exhaustion.

Suddenly, Matt's head shot up. "Ice cream time? Who wants the best ice cream in town?" He fanned his damp shirt, trying to cool off.

Jack's face lit up. "Count me in!"

Without missing a beat, Noah zipped his dusty bat bag. "Me too! Best plan ever. I want the biggest ice cream cone they have."

The idea was a good one. The Owls moved with a burst of fresh energy; their feet weren't so tired anymore. They crowded out of the dugout chatting and laughing as they marched to get their refreshing sweets. At the Tasty Treat, they got their ice creams and sat at a big picnic table.

Noah let out a long sigh, his shoulders slumping like he'd just struck out. "I was off today at practice," he mumbled, scuffing his shoe against the ground. "Couldn't stop thinking about playing the Lizards. They're tough, and I just can't shake off this weird feeling about playing them again. I really don't like them at all."

Jack's smile disappeared as Noah trash-talked the Lizards. He glanced down at his phone, pretending not to listen.

Noah licked the dripping ice cream on his cone and then glanced up. "Hey Jack, aren't the Lizards from your old town? Do you know them?"

"Yeah," Jack said quietly, giving a small, almost invisible, nod.

Noah's voice dropped as he said, "Well, let me tell you. Last year, they crushed us. And their best pitcher, Preston Jones, is back. That dude struck me out five out of five times. I hate to say it, but it'll probably be the same thing tomorrow. We just can't beat them." He sighed as he watched another blob of ice cream fall from his cone.

Matt bit into his cone, his eyes shining. "Hey, like Coach Wolf said, it's a new season."

"Doesn't matter," Noah interrupted. "We don't stand a chance, to be honest. They're just too good. They always win. Maybe there's a trick to it, like some of their kids are too old or the umps are on their side." He chomped on the last bit of cone. "They don't say it, but you can tell they think they're the best. It bugs me."

Chase, their right fielder, crumpled his napkin, frowning like Noah. "Yeah, I'm not a fan either," he said.

Jack's stomach dropped, and he stood up, walking to the trash can to avoid the conversation.

Groaning, Noah slumped against the table. "And we're playing them first, just our luck! It figures."

JJ, their star pitcher, chimed in, "I know one thing. They can really swing the bats. I can't get my best fastball by them."

6

"Yep, and that's why we don't stand a chance." Noah sulked. Suddenly, his eyes lit up with an idea. "What if we just ignore them tomorrow? No talking, no looking at them, nothing. Let's show them we don't like them."

Chase nodded eagerly. "Count me in." The other Owls murmured their agreement, except for Jack and Matt, who shared a brief, uncertain look.

Standing up, Matt brushed crumbs off his shirt. "Time to head home," he said, glancing at Jack. "You coming?" Jack nodded, and they waved goodbye to the rest of the Owls.

They walked in silence. Jack, usually chatty and relaxed, stared ahead, his eyebrows furrowed.

"You're quiet. What's up?" Matt asked as they passed the corner store.

Jack stopped in his tracks, biting his lower lip. "Can I ask you something?"

"Let's hear it."

"Do you think the L-Burg players are bad guys?" Jack asked, his voice barely more than a whisper.

Matt shrugged like it was no big deal. "Not really. Why? Sure, they beat us, but they were good sports about it."

"Remember when Noah asked if I knew the Lizards?" Jack's eyes searched for Matt's reaction.

"Yeah?" Matt leaned in, his eyes wide with curiosity.

Jack let out a deep sigh. "I do know those guys. They're actually my friends. We went to school together. Last year, I couldn't play for them because I hurt my wrist. By the time it healed, the only team with a roster spot was the West Salem Wildcats. If my family hadn't moved to Oak Grove, I'd be wearing a Lizard jersey this season."

"Wow, so you really *do* know them!" Matt said, surprised.

Jack nodded and started walking again, his shoes dragging on the sidewalk. "Yeah, they're great guys, and we still hang out and play video games together. Noah has it all wrong. I should have said something, but I didn't want him and the other guys to get mad."

"Don't worry about them," Matt said, kicking a pebble with his foot. "They can be sore losers sometimes. Coach Wolf has been clear on good sportsmanship, and they've got some growing up to do."

The boys made it to Jack's house. The warm light from the living room spilled out onto the porch. "Thanks, Matt," Jack said with a small smile. "You're the best. See you tomorrow morning."

"See you tomorrow! And hey, just ignore what Noah said." Jack held out his fist, and Matt bumped it before turning and continuing his walk home. Jack watched him go, his friend getting smaller and smaller in the dim light of the streetlights.

When Matt turned the corner, Jack stepped inside and dropped his bag. The smell of dinner filled the air, and his mouth watered. Jack's dad looked up from his glowing tablet with a smile. "How'd practice go? Know anything about the tournament tomorrow?"

Jack shrugged. "It was alright, I guess. Coach says our game is at ten tomorrow. We gotta be there by nine. What's for dinner?"

His dad, smiling, answered, "Your mom made lasagna. C'mon in and we'll eat."

As Jack slid into his chair next to his mom, his dad asked, "Who's your first game against?"

"The Lizards," Jack said, his voice wavering as he scooped the steaming lasagna onto his plate.

His dad's face lit up. "No way! Really? Must be kind of weird for you, right? Playing against your friends, I mean."

Jack nodded a little. The lasagna no longer looked as appetizing as he thought about tomorrow's game. He fiddled with the noodles.

His mom's face brightened. "We'll get to catch up with all their parents. We haven't seen most of them since we moved to Oak Grove. Tomorrow will be so much fun!"

Jack nodded. He really missed hanging out with his old friends and couldn't wait to see them. But now, he was an Owl, and Noah made it clear that the Lizards were the enemy. Tomorrow didn't seem like it was going to be a fun day.

You're Up to Bat!

Jack says it's your turn to shine! Answering the questions helps you score runs. Answer one question? That's a single. Two? You've got a double. Three gets you a triple; four is a home run, and all five? You've hit a grand slam! Let's swing for the fences!

Chapter 1

1. How do you think Jack feels playing against his old team?

2. How would you feel playing against your friends?

3. Why should we not judge others, like the L-Burg players, without really knowing them?

4. If you were facing a team that always beat you, like the Lizards, how would you prepare?

5. How do you feel when you don't know what will happen in a game? What helps you feel better?

2

Storm Clouds Over the Diamond

"Jack, buddy, wake up! It's game day!" Jack's dad's voice echoed down the hallway.

Jack was already awake, staring at the ceiling. His thoughts were like a jumbled deck of baseball cards. "I'm up!" he croaked, peeling the sheets off and trudging towards the shower.

"Remember, be at Shally Field by nine. Big day ahead!" his dad called.

Jack didn't need the reminder. He had tossed and turned all night, thinking about the game. His mind flooded with questions. *What's it going to be like playing against my friends? Will I play okay? What about Noah and the rest of the guys? What if they figure out that I'm friends with the Lizards?*

Stepping out of the shower, Jack slid into his gray Owls uniform, fumbling with his belt, and missing a few buttons on the jersey. The green Owl patch still looked fierce, but Jack couldn't muster the enthusiasm to copy the piercing look. The fabric clung to him as his mind jumped between uncertainty and excitement.

***

The sky was gray, which didn't help his mood. Jack dragged his feet as he headed out the door and followed the damp sidewalk to the field. His mind was full of thoughts, making his bag feel heavier than it really was.

It's supposed to be sunny during baseball season, Jack thought to himself. He turned the last corner, and the field came into view. Cheers from the first game of the morning cut through the light mist.

Scanning his surroundings, Jack spotted a group of Lizards players huddled at the far end of the parking lot. Even clustered together in their green and gold uniforms, their faces and voices were easily recognizable. The laughter echoing from the group tugged a half-smile from Jack. His smile didn't last long. A group text from Noah buzzed in his pocket.

Remember Owls. Ignore the Lizards! Let them know we don't like them!

Jack's stomach twisted. He ducked behind some trees, peering out to make sure none of the Lizards saw him. He was on a new team now and didn't want to seem disloyal.

"Hey, Jack! Playing hide and seek?" called a voice behind him. It was his best friend Alex, the shortstop for the Lizards. Alex put his arm around Jack's shoulder. "I kept texting you last night. Why didn't you answer?"

Jack's shoulders tensed up. "Alex! I just got…uh…busy," he stuttered, his words tumbling out in a nervous rush. He glanced around, searching for any Owls lurking nearby.

Alex's eyes lit up as he playfully slapped Jack's back. "Imagine if you hadn't moved. You'd be a Lizard right now. We'd be unstoppable with you at third and me at short!" Alex's grin spread from ear to ear. "How've you been? How do you like your new team?"

"I'm good. The team's okay," Jack answered hurriedly. His heart skipped a beat when he saw Noah and the other Owls sitting atop the bleachers, staring at him. "Um, I should…uh…check in with my coach. I gotta go." Alex's smile faded as Jack backed away.

"Oh, okay…" Alex mumbled, his disappointment clear in his quiet voice. His mouth opened to say more, but the words faded on his lips as Jack disappeared into the crowd.

Jack tiptoed between the bleachers, trying to avoid the Owls' prying eyes.

Just act natural, he thought as he quickly sat down in the first row of still-damp bleachers.

"Act like you're watching the game," he whispered, leaning in to see the field better. He nervously fidgeted with his phone, sitting stiffly. Suddenly, he felt someone near him.

"Hey, what was that about?" Noah sneered, standing over him. "Didn't you get my text?"

Jack's heart pounded, and his cheeks warmed, but he spoke calmly. "Look, I used to go to school with them. They're still my friends. Sorry, but I'm not going to ignore them just because you say so. And by the way, they're good guys."

"Fine, do what you want. I don't care," Noah snapped. "The other guys will see whose side you're really on. You might as well be wearing green and gold today."

Before Jack could reply, Noah turned and marched toward the other Owls. Their eyes fixed on Jack as if he was their favorite TV show.

Jack took a few deep breaths to calm himself down. He knew it was right to speak up, but he still felt uneasy. Then, someone put a hand on his shoulder. "Morning, Jack! Ready for the game?"

"Hi, Matt. Yeah, I guess. Umm… Noah just got mad at me 'cause I talked to a Lizard," Jack blurted out. "I told him they're my friends, and he didn't like it."

"Noah's something else. I'm glad you stood up to him. You were loyal to your friends," Matt said, nodding in approval. "Let's just focus on the game now. It's going to be tough, and we need to be ready to play our best."

"I'll be ready," Jack said with a forced smile.

The first game ended, and Jack, Matt, and the rest of the Owls carried their gear through the gate toward the emptying first-base dugout. Jack plopped his bat bag against the chain-link fence with a clank and pulled out his glove.

15

"Hi, Chase. Hi, Jordan." Jack waved as he passed the boys on his way to warm up with Matt. Jordan said a quick 'Hey' but didn't look at him. Chase stayed silent.

Great, just great. They're mad at me, Jack thought, his lips pressed tightly together.

Suddenly, the sky, which had been threatening all morning, finally let a few raindrops fall.

It's going to be one of those days, Jack thought as he sighed and began throwing with Matt.

"Okay, boys, bring it in!" Coach Wolf called, waving his arm at the group. He stared worriedly at the ever-darkening sky, his eyebrows raised. The Owls dashed for the dugout, weaving through the rain as if dodging sprinkler drops.

Coach Wolf brushed a few raindrops off his jacket. "Before we start, I have a few things to say. First, we won the toss and we're the home team. Let's play with energy in this first inning and get off to a good start. Second, the Lizards aren't starting their best pitcher, Preston Jones."

"Why's he out?" asked Drew Dawson, the Owls' second baseman.

"Can't say," replied Coach Wolf with a shrug.

"They know they're going to beat us without him. Hey, maybe we'll get rained out. That's our only hope," Noah mumbled. He looked at his nearby teammates, who, judging by their gloomy faces, all seemed to agree.

"Last thing, the weather isn't looking great. Heavier rain might be on its way," Coach Wolf said. Noah tilted his head and glanced at Chase, barely hiding a smirk.

Across the diamond, the Lizards chattered excitedly. They bounced on their toes, the eagerness to play spilling from the dugout. L-Burg's bright gold shirts stood out against the muddy infield. Most Owls, thinking the game was already lost, shuffled slowly to their positions in the field as heavier raindrops greeted them.

Jack reached third base and looked at his teammates. *We're not going to beat anyone with this kind of attitude*, he thought.

JJ was on the mound, tossing his last few pitches. His fastballs zipped through the air but never hit their target. His curveballs were just as bad. Cooper, behind the plate, huffed as he wiped off the mud-caked balls, his face scrunching with each wild warm-up pitch.

"C'mon, JJ, throw strikes, will ya? Let's find the plate," the catcher said, picking up another dirty ball and sending it back to the pitcher with a lazy toss. Even the mild-mannered Cooper's mood had soured.

Jack, standing at third base, waited for Noah to throw him a grounder. It didn't happen. Noah ignored him and just threw warm-up balls to Danny at shortstop and Drew at second. Noah shot Jack a mean look. Jack quickly looked away, holding his head up high.

Jack clenched his jaw. He wanted to yell across the diamond, but didn't. Instead, he took some deep breaths and tried to focus on the game.

"Play ball!" the umpire shouted, and the Lizards' first hitter confidently marched to the plate.

JJ's wildness continued. First one ball, then two, then three. With each pitch, JJ's frown grew deeper, and his shoulders sagged further. Every time Cooper threw the ball back, he let out an enormous sigh, shaking his head as if he couldn't believe what was happening.

Jack noticed his pitcher struggle from third base. "You got this! Make your pitch! You can do it!" he shouted, slapping his now damp glove with a steady rhythm.

Jack's encouragement didn't seem to help. JJ paced near the mound, shaking his head. Jack could hear the pitcher muttering, "Don't walk the first batter. Whatever you do, don't walk this guy. Don't throw another ball."

JJ stepped on the pitching rubber, looking in at Cooper. Struggling with the wet ball, the tall right-hander fired a fastball towards home.

"Ball four, take your base!" The umpire's voice rang out, and he pointed towards first base.

Noah sighed heavily and kicked at a clump of mud. He looked over to the Owls' second baseman, Drew. "Great start, huh? It's going to be a long day. I told you we'd lose," he whined. Drew looked down at his feet, his face hidden by his cap.

JJ caught Noah's words and his stare back was as sharp as a line drive.

"Do you want to pitch? Do you?" the tall pitcher snapped. The frustration was clear in his voice.

"Well, throw strikes, will ya?" Noah muttered over his shoulder, walking back to first base.

JJ's pitches kept dancing around the strike zone and he walked the next two Lizards, filling the bases. Cooper called time out. He and the other Owls infielders, except for Noah, headed for a meeting with JJ. Jack motioned to Noah, but he stayed at first, arms crossed and eyebrows pulled together.

As he got closer to the mound, Jack heard JJ say, "Bases loaded, and it's all my fault. I can't do it. Why can't I just throw strikes? I'm a terrible pitcher."

Jack reached out and tapped his tall pitcher's leg. "Hey, you're not a terrible pitcher! Don't say that. You're as good as anyone. We'll get out of this." JJ just frowned. Jack's encouraging words bounced off the pitcher like raindrops on the dugout roof.

As he headed back to third base, Jack noticed Noah's scowl and JJ nervously pacing by the mound. *Everything's going wrong today. Noah's pouting at first. Our pitcher doesn't have confidence. We're in trouble. This is not going to be good.*

As Jack feared, the situation was about to become even more challenging for JJ and the Owls.

All eyes were on Tanner Goodsaint as the Lizards' cleanup hitter confidently walked towards home plate. He towered over

Cooper, the Owls catcher, and could look eye-to-eye with the home plate umpire. Pitchers feared him for good reason. His powerful swing had sent many baseballs sailing over the fence. Matt motioned to the other Owls' outfielders to take a few steps back.

The Lizards' dangerous hitter adjusted his batting gloves. Cooper, standing beside home plate, felt the strong breeze from his powerful warmup swings. With determination written all over his face, Tanner dug into the muddy batter's box.

JJ nervously rubbed the side of his face and peered into the Owls' dugout.

"You're okay! Make your pitch! Everyone, on your toes!" Coach Wolf yelled, nervously chewing his gum.

JJ's first pitch, a fastball, was a gem, hitting the outside corner at the knees.

"Ball one," the umpire declared confidently.

Jack's eyes widened as a wave of groans rolled from the Owls' fans, some even peering out from their umbrellas to shout their dismay.

JJ shook his head in disbelief, his mouth falling open. "That was right there! Are you kidding me? What does it take to get a strike called?" He slammed the now-darkened baseball into his glove. Clenching his jaw, JJ hurled the next pitch right down the middle, aiming for perfection. It was a pitch he wished he could get back.

Crack!

The ball soared off the hitter's bat and screamed skyward. The Owls' fans gasped; a sound overpowered by loud cheers from the Lizards' crowd. Slicing through the raindrops, the baseball seemed to pick up speed as it escaped the ballpark. A grand slam.

Jack's shoulders dropped as he watched Alex and the Lizards celebrate the blast. He glanced over at Noah, who tossed his arms up in the air, still complaining to Drew at second base.

The inning got worse. Coach Wolf pulled JJ from the mound, but the Lizards kept finding their way on base. Walks, solid base hits, and Owls' errors, it didn't matter. By the time the inning ended, the red glow from the scoreboard revealed that seven L-burg runners had trampled on home plate.

The rain picked up, and the Owls trudged off the field. Their shoes sank in the mud, just like their spirits. In frustration, Noah tossed his glove against the dugout wall, almost hitting one of the other players.

"He's lucky Coach Wolf didn't catch that," Jack whispered to Matt, who shook his head. The team sat quietly, watching L-Burg excitedly sprint onto the field.

Drew led off the inning for the Owls with Noah and Danny to follow.

"I told you they'd beat us, right?" whined Noah to no one in particular. He slid his helmet on, grabbed his bat, and slowly made his way to the on-deck circle. "It doesn't matter what we do. The game's over already."

What an attitude, Jack thought, watching the pouting Owls' first baseman kick at some mud.

"Playing in the rain? How can anyone hit with a wet bat?" Noah grumbled, before he took a few lazy swings. "Who cares? I'll probably get out, anyway."

After Drew struck out on a 2-2 pitch, Noah slowly walked to the plate. The rain got heavier and tiny puddles formed outside the dugout. Noah tried wiping the raindrops off his bat, but like the game, it was a losing battle.

The first pitch to Noah was at the knees on the inside corner. He jumped back, as if playing dodge ball.

"Strike one!" called out the umpire.

Noah shook his head, sighed loudly, and smacked his cleats with his bat. Some mud splattered on his pant leg. He squinted his eyes, and his lips pressed together.

The next pitch was a change-up that bounced on the ground in front of the plate. Noah swung wildly, losing his footing, and almost tumbling over. Some Owls couldn't help but chuckle, and even Jack smirked.

At least there's something to smile about, he thought.

The redness in Noah's cheeks deepened as he dug in with his back foot. The next pitch was straight down the middle, but Noah didn't move.

"Steeerike three!" the umpire shouted, his right arm punching the air.

"No way!" Noah grumbled under his breath, his face scrunching up like a used paper bag. As he walked into the dugout, he grunted, "That was too low, not a strike. See, I told you, the umps want them to win."

After Noah walked past, a now-smiling Jack whispered to Matt, "That was definitely a strike."

"Yep, right down the middle. Gotta swing with two strikes," Matt noted, sounding like a wise baseball coach.

After Danny's short fly ended the inning, the rain slowed to a drizzle, but darker clouds were rolling in. The Owls' spirits matched the graying skies. They plodded to their positions. A still-pouting Noah didn't even bother to bring out a ball to throw infield practice.

Oh, come on, Noah! Jack thought, shaking his head.

Coach Wolf, hands on his hips, stared out at the field. "Hustle out there! Let's go!"

The Owls tried to muster smiles and look excited. But their smiles were crooked, and their brief burst of energy faded.

Calvin James, the first L-burg batter, hit a sharp single to left field. It skipped right through Jordan's legs and kept going. Jordan just stood there, arms up, not turning to chase the baseball. By the time Matt threw the ball back to the infield, the speedy Lizard rounded the bases.

Just then, the day's darkest clouds dumped huge raindrops on Shally Field, making fans run for cover. A crack of thunder rumbled in the distance. The umpire quickly waved the players off the field. The Owls ran to the dugout, showing more energy than they had all day.

Soon, the infield turned into a little lake. Everyone knew there would be no more baseball played today.

The wet Owls moved around each other in silence, slowly gathering their gear in the dugout. Shouts of laughter cut through the rain. The Owls looked across the diamond and saw the Lizards joking and high fiving as they packed up.

"Hold up!" Coach Wolf bellowed. The players froze, turning towards him. "What I saw today wasn't good." His voice was heavy with disappointment. "No energy, poor attitudes, and poor sportsmanship."

Coach Wolf continued, "You weren't good teammates. That's not how we win games, and that is not who we are. We'll have a lot to talk about at Wednesday's practice." With a deep sigh, Coach Wolf turned and walked away. The boys packed away their equipment without uttering a word.

It was a quiet ride home for Jack. His eyes followed each drop of rain racing down the car window. The only sound was the swish of the windshield wipers battling the steady rain. His dad said something, but Jack didn't hear him. His mind was far away, replaying the day's game against the Lizards. He realized today was a washout … in more ways than one.

You're Up to Bat!

Jack says it's your turn to shine! Answering the questions helps you score runs. Answer one question? That's a single. Two? You've got a double. Three gets you a triple; four is a home run, and all five? You've hit a grand slam! Let's swing for the fences!

Chapter 2

1. Jack had a lot of questions in his mind before the game. What do you think about before a big game?

2. Jack had to deal with Noah being mad at him. How would you handle a teammate who was upset with you?

3. Noah had a negative attitude during the game. How does one person's mood affect the whole team?

4. What wouldn't you like if you were Coach Wolf watching the game?

5. The game didn't go as planned for the Owls. What helps you feel better after a tough game?

3

The Owls' Game Plan:
Win One Pitch at a Time

The rain played a gentle rhythm on Jack's bedroom window, like a soft drumbeat. Everywhere in his room were reminders of his love of baseball. Posters of his baseball heroes, frozen in action as they swung their bats, hung on the walls. Shiny rings and trophies, each one reminding him of past victories, covered the top of his dresser.

Jack stretched out on his bed, sending a baseball into the air and catching it again and again, each toss filled with thoughts of the day's game. The Owls didn't play well. His cheeks puffed out as he blew a big breath.

We need something, but what?

His phone buzzed and interrupted his thoughts. Alex, his best friend from the Lizards, was calling. Jack sat up, hesitating, before he answered.

"Tough game today, huh, Jack?" Alex asked, his voice full of sympathy.

Jack sighed, his shoulders slumping like a deflated balloon. "Yeah, we were off. Way off."

Alex paused. "Yeah, you guys seemed lost today."

Jack sat up straighter. "We just couldn't get it together. It's like we lost the game before we even started. I think we need help, but not just with our hitting and fielding. It's something else…"

"You mean the mental game?" Alex asked.

"Exactly. You guys always seem so focused, so together. How do you do it?"

Alex chuckled. "You know my dad is our coach, right? He's big on teaching us the mental game. He learned about it when he played professional baseball. We do mental game training a lot. It's kind of like our super-power. It helps us to stay focused, keep our cool under pressure, and playing hard no matter what!"

Jack perked up, admiring how Alex always seemed to have an inside scoop. "Mental game training? That's exactly what we need. I wish we had a coach for that."

Everything went quiet, and then Alex said, "Hold on," and put down the phone.

Jack waited, playing with the baseball. After a long time, Alex came back on the phone.

"Okay, so I talked to my dad. He loves teaching the mental game and said he'd be happy to help your team. He knows Coach Wolf and will call him."

Jack felt a wave of relief and excitement. "That's amazing, Alex! Thanks! This could really change everything."

"Happy to help, buddy. Tell your teammates to hang in there. I look forward to seeing you at another tournament," Alex said, before hanging up.

Jack plopped his head back on the pillow. *This might just save our season,* he thought.

***

On Wednesday, the Owls met for practice. Their faces were gloomy. They glanced at each other, but nobody said a word, all still focused on Saturday's terrible game.

Suddenly, Coach Wolf clapped his hands loudly. It broke the quiet and made everyone jump.

Eyeing each player, he said, "Okay, Owls! Saturday's game with the Lizards was tough. We made mistakes in hitting, pitching, and catching. But the biggest mistake was how we played mentally. It seemed like our heads just weren't in the game. We lost our focus, our energy dipped, and we didn't work together as a team."

Their eyes fell, and their shoulders slumped. They knew their coach was right.

"We can fix this. Remember, champions learn from their mistakes. So, today's practice will be different. No hitting, throwing, or fielding. Just leave your bags here and come with me to the pavilion." The boys glanced at each other, confused.

We must be going to work on our mental game, Jack thought, trying to contain his excitement.

Cooper whispered to Noah as they followed the coach, "What's going on?"

Noah stretched his neck to see better. "Not sure, but there's someone with a whiteboard. Looks like school," he said with a shrug. Cooper almost stumbled as he tried to get a better look.

Jack's smile got even bigger as he kept his guess about the surprise to himself.

As they walked closer to the pavilion, the boys leaned in, whispering and wide-eyed with growing curiosity. Standing before them was a tall, muscular man in a well-worn baseball cap, smiling broadly. It was someone they recognized.

The Owls scrambled to sit down at the picnic tables, looking at each other and their visitor.

Coach Wolf gave a friendly pat on the tall man's shoulder. "Boys, this is Jerick Ranger. He's the coach of the Lattasburg Lizards. You saw him on Saturday. We played baseball together in college. Jerick even played pro baseball later."

"The Lizards? Really?" Noah muttered under his breath. His searching eyes found Jack, who quickly glanced away.

Coach Wolf's gaze swept the team as he said, "Coach Ranger is here to help us play better. Being good at baseball isn't just about hitting, catching, and throwing. There's another big part—the mental game. It's all about how you think, feel, and act when you play, especially in between the pitches."

"Mental game? Like, mind tricks?" Jordan asked, scratching his head.

Coach Wolf laughed a little. "It's not mind tricks. It's about learning ways to stay sharp, deal with pressure, and play your best in any situation. That's what we need."

Jack watched his teammates' faces go from confused to interested. Even Noah, who seemed grumpy, now looked curious. He leaned to Matt and whispered, "This is like the deep breathing, the 3 Ts, and the pre-pitch stuff you showed me, right?"

Matt nodded. "Yep, it's about getting ready for the next pitch. I only taught you a little about the mental game. There's a lot more to learn if we want to be great players."

As the Owls introduced themselves to Coach Ranger, Jack felt enthusiastic. *Matt's right. We have a lot more to learn. I can't wait!*

"Thank you, Coach! Hi, Owls!" Mr. Ranger said, smiling big. "Wow, look at the grass stains on your pants. I can see you've been working hard on the field. But, like Coach Wolf said, there's another secret to winning. It's having a great mental game."

31

The Lizards' coach playfully tossed and caught a baseball. "Usually, players learn about the mental game in high school or college. But today, you'll learn these secrets."

He paused, letting the words sink in. "I'll show you how to stay focused, reset after mistakes, and play baseball one pitch at a time."

Coach Ranger walked to the whiteboard, marker in hand, and declared, "This is always the most important goal when you play baseball."

The players leaned in, wide-eyed and eager. He wrote in big, bold letters. Stepping back, the board read:

Your Big Goal: Win the Next Pitch!

"Baseball," he declared, "is all about being ready for the next pitch. It's a game of stop and go. You pitch, then wait. Pitch again and wait again. Often in one game, there are over 100 of these pitches and pauses."

"Focus on playing one pitch at a time. Think of each pitch as a mini-game. Each one is a new chance for something good to happen. The next pitch is the most important pitch in any game. It doesn't matter what just happened. It's all about resetting and winning that next pitch. Win the pitch, and you win the at-bat. Win at-bats, and you win innings. Win innings, and you win the game."

"Here's the secret," Coach Ranger said with a wink. "What you do between pitches is super important. Using mental game skills gets you really ready to win that next pitch."

Jack's hand shot up in the air. "Ah, so, it's all about the next pitch. If I mess up on one pitch, I need to shake it off fast and just get ready for the next one?"

"That's it, Jack! Each pitch is a new chance to show what you can do. How many of you have had two strikes and still got a hit? How many of you pitchers have been 3-0 and still got the batter out?" asked Coach Ranger.

The boys looked at each other, and soon every hand went up.

"Right! You've all succeeded before in those situations. So, even with two strikes when batting or a 3-0 count when pitching, don't panic. Something good can always happen on the next pitch. That's the way you should think. Keep the game simple: play one pitch at a time. The next pitch is always the most important pitch in any game. Just focus on winning that next pitch!"

The boys glanced at each other, their heads bobbing in understanding.

Coach Ranger looked around. "When it's only you and the next pitch, you're at your best. How does that feel?"

"I'm ready! I'm having fun and not worrying about anything. It's all about that pitch," Jack said, his eyes sparkling with excitement. "I'm also full of energy and on my toes."

"I feel confident and relaxed," Matt added, his voice perking up.

Cooper said, "The crowd noise fades away, sounding far off, just like background music. I'm not really thinking about anything. My focus is sharp and only on the baseball, with no distractions. It's like I'm zooming through a level in my video game."

Jack chuckled, shaking his head. "That's Cooper, always thinking about video games."

"Anyone else?" the coach encouraged.

Noah, looking amazed, swung his hands like he was hitting a ball. "It might sound weird, but the ball looks bigger, and it's like everything slows down. I can see it all the way from the pitcher's hand to my bat."

"Fantastic! You've all described being super focused, confident, and not overthinking. You're playing one pitch at a time, and that means your mind is in the right place. All players have that happen once in a while. But I'll show you how to have that same focus before every pitch of every inning of every game," Coach Ranger said, looking excited.

The coach asked, "Before we learn each of the actual mental game skills, can anyone say what we've learned so far?"

Matt leaned forward and his hand zoomed up. "Baseball is a game of pitches and breaks. Each pitch, no matter what the count, is a new chance to succeed. Don't worry about the whole game. Just try to win this *next* pitch. You're going to teach us mental game skills to help us get better at doing just that."

"You get an 'A'! Great job, Matt." Coach Ranger grinned. "Now that we know winning the next pitch is the goal, let's learn each of the skills." The team looked at each other, determined and ready.

Jack watched his team, a smile creeping across his face. *This is exactly what we needed. I can see the excitement in everyone's eyes, even Noah's. Baseball is about taking it one pitch at a time. The next pitch is always the most important, so we have to be ready for it!*

You're Up to Bat!

Jack says it's your turn to shine! Answering the questions helps you score runs. Answer one question? That's a single. Two? You've got a double. Three gets you a triple; four is a home run, and all five? You've hit a grand slam! Let's swing for the fences!

Chapter 3

1. How does it feel to talk about a tough game with a friend?

2. What do you think is the most important pitch in a game?

3. Coach Ranger says each pitch is like a mini game. What does that mean to you?

4. How would you explain 'one pitch at a time' to a friend? A parent or coach? Explain it to someone.

5. What's a new tip you want to try from this chapter in your next game?

4

The First Three Puzzle Pieces

The pavilion was alive with excitement. Coach Ranger had just taught the Owls a new baseball secret: **it's all about being ready to win the next pitch. Win the pitch, win the at-bat. Win at-bats, win innings. Win innings, win games!** But the Owls still had some questions.

Jack scratched his head. "I get that the next pitch is always the most important pitch of the game, but what exactly can we do to get ready for it?"

Coach Ranger said with a wide smile, "It's all about learning different mental game skills. Think of them like puzzle pieces in the big 'Win the Next Pitch!' puzzle. We'll learn the pieces one by one and then put them all together. Let's get started." He led the boys to a large table in front of the pavilion.

Pointing at the table, he said, "Here are seven puzzle pieces, each for a different mental game skill. They're easy to learn but need practice. Let's flip them over one by one and talk about each. Who wants to pick the first one?"

Hands shot up like rockets, and the boys bounced on their toes, beaming with anticipation.

With a warm smile, Coach Ranger turned to Drew. "You pick the first one!"

Drew carefully looked over the pieces, picked one, and flipped it over. "**Keep Learning**," he called out, his voice echoing throughout the pavilion.

"'Keep Learning.' What an awesome piece to start with!" Coach Ranger said, clapping his hands with excitement. "There's so much to learn about playing baseball. Did you know that even professional baseball players never stop learning? They might be amazing at hitting home runs or throwing lightning-fast pitches, but they still have coaches who teach them new things every single day. Pro players are like sponges, always soaking up knowledge. That is what each of you needs to do."

Coach Ranger turned to the whiteboard and wrote: **Learn Something New Every Day!**

"Just like the pros, your goal is to learn as much as you can," he continued. "You can learn how to improve your swing, play better on defense, and even understand baseball strategy better. Finally, you also need to keep learning about yourself as a player. Pay attention to exactly what you are doing and feeling when you're playing your very best."

The coach looked around at the eager faces. "Coaches teach us new things, but how else can we keep learning about baseball?"

Drew's hand shot up. "I watch other players play on TV or at the baseball field. I also watch videos online. You can learn a lot from seeing what other players do."

"I read books about baseball. That's how I learned some cool things about catching," Cooper chimed in.

JJ added, "I ask my older brother about pitching. He's pitches on the high school team, and he shows me stuff."

"Excellent, boys! You're on the right track," Coach Ranger said with a nod. "Besides someone teaching you, how else can you learn about baseball?"

The boys put their heads together, thinking hard, until Matt finally said, "What about learning from our mistakes? Like when I mess up, I try to figure out what I did wrong so I can do better next time."

"Fantastic answer, Matt!" Coach Ranger exclaimed. "Some of the most important lessons come from mistakes. We try something, it doesn't work, and then we try something else. But here's a secret: it's just as important to learn from what we do right! We can learn a lot from playing well, too."

I never thought about that, Jack thought, his eyes wide. *If I do something right, I need to remind myself after practice or the game, so I can do it that way again.*

Coach Ranger sat down and motioned to Coach Wolf. "I believe you have something special for these young ballplayers."

"I sure do!" Coach Wolf grinned and reached into his bag, pulling out small notebooks with the Owls' logo and each player's name and number.

"We're going to use these notebooks this season," Coach Wolf explained, handing them out one by one. The boys eagerly accepted them. "After every practice or game," Coach Wolf continued, "you'll write at least one thing you've learned about yourself or the game of baseball. If you learn more, that's even better. Then, at the start of our next practice, you can share what you've discovered because it might help one of your teammates."

Jack flipped through his notebook, already imagining the lessons he would write. "This is such a cool idea, Matt! I hope I fill this whole thing up by the end of the season!"

Matt flashed a toothy smile. "Me too!"

Coach Ranger stood tall and pulled a worn notebook from his pocket, holding it out to the Owls. "See, even we coaches use one of these. We're always learning too, right?"

Coach Wolf chimed in, reaching into his back pocket to pull out his notebook. "You bet. I've got mine right here!"

A rush of chatter filled the pavilion as the Owls started talking about their new notebooks and how they'd learn something new every day.

Coach Ranger fit the '**Keep Learning**' piece into the puzzle. "One down, six to go," he announced.

"Okay, Jack. Your turn." Coach Ranger said. Jack picked up the closest piece.

His eyes lit up. "**Energy!**" he shouted, handing the piece to Coach Ranger.

The coach beamed. "Energy—perfect! High energy is key to playing your best."

He reached into his bag and pulled out a large cardboard cutout, an Energy Meter. It had a red end marked 'Low', a yellow middle, and a green end marked 'High', with a big pointer at the center.

ENERGY METER

Play with High Energy !

Coach Ranger held the meter high. "This shows your team's energy in a game," he said. "It changes based on what you do. Think back to the Lizards game. Where was your energy on this meter?"

The Owls fell silent, ducking their heads. A few of them mumbled, "Low."

Coach Ranger moved the pointer down to the red zone.

Coach Wolf nodded. "Yep, our team's energy was in the red. What made our energy go so low?"

Jack noticed Noah sigh deeply and look down, remembering last Saturday's game.

Noah raised his hand. "Before the game, I was already low on energy, thinking we'd lose. I wanted to give up before we started. Moping definitely didn't help our energy."

Amazed by Noah's honesty, Jack whispered to himself, "He's getting interested in this mental game stuff."

Cooper played with his cap, and his face scrunched. "We were too tough on each other. I shouted at JJ to pitch better, and it just made everything worse. That didn't help the team's energy."

Frowning, Noah added, "I yelled at our pitcher too. Also, I didn't hustle out to the field, and I didn't even bring out an infield ball. All those things lowered the energy." He shook his head, regretfully.

"Good job noticing that, Noah," Coach Wolf said with a warm smile. "Who else has something to share?"

Jordan glanced at the ground. "I sure let our energy drop when I pouted and didn't chase a ball in left field."

Coach Ranger nodded. "Your examples show how the Energy Meter can hit red. Bad energy spreads fast, but good energy spreads faster! So, what can we do to boost our energy?"

Ideas started flying.

Jack's hand shot up again. "We're energized when we cheer for each other, like after a nice hit or an awesome catch!"

"Absolutely right!" Coach Ranger agreed, clapping his hands. "Rooting for each other means we're all in this together. That moves our energy arrow towards the green." He slid the arrow from red to yellow. "What else can we do?"

Matt spoke up. "Pick each other up after a mistake. Let your teammates know you're there for them. Say something like, 'You'll get it next time!'"

Coach Ranger's smile widened. "Exactly! Supporting each other, especially after mistakes, keeps the Energy Meter in the green."

With a curious tilt of his head, the coach asked, "Does anyone know how body language affects the Energy Meter?"

The Owls paused to think. After a moment, Cooper, the team's catcher, answered, "Your body says a lot about your attitude. No matter what is happening, you need to stand tall and look ready, not slumped with your head down. Good body language is like saying, 'We're still in this game!'"

"That's right, Cooper!" the coach exclaimed. "Your body language says a lot about your energy level. Heads hanging and shoulders sagging, shout, 'It's no use! We're done!' It really drags the Energy Meter down into the red."

"How did you know that?" Coach Ranger asked, putting his hand on his chin.

A crease formed between Cooper's eyebrows. "Well, after the game, my dad told me my body language wasn't great. He noticed I was sighing, moping, and shaking my head after each bad pitch. My dad said that didn't help my pitcher's confidence. He said my terrible body language doesn't just bring me down, it brings everyone down."

Coach Ranger added, "He's right. Catchers, you're on center stage after every pitch. Your teammates are watching you closely to see your reaction. Be a leader and set the tone with positive body language. All these things—cheering, supporting, and staying positive—they don't just push our Energy Meter to green. They keep it there all game long!"

The coach went on, "So, boys, **Energy** is an important piece of the 'Win the Next Pitch' puzzle. **Make sure you play with a lot of energy on every pitch. Everyone plays a part in keeping our Energy Meter green. During the game, check your energy. Ask yourself, 'Am I helping or hurting our team's energy?'"**

"Are you guys ready to keep your Energy Meter green all the time?" asked Coach Wolf.

"Yes!" The Owls yelled, giving each other fist bumps and high fives.

Coach Ranger lifted the Energy Meter high above his head, his voice booming with excitement. "Awesome!" The boys laughed as he zoomed the Energy Meter's arrow into the green.

Play with High Energy !

"I'm giving this Energy Meter to Coach Wolf. He'll hang it in the dugout and change it during games. That way, we can all keep an eye on our energy level," Coach Ranger said, passing it to Coach Wolf.

Jack squinted thoughtfully, rubbing his chin. *If we all keep our own energy up, then our team's Energy Meter stays green. That's important to remember!*

"So, let's see what's next," Coach Ranger said as he eyed the other pieces on the table.

The Owls leaned in around the table again, each studying the remaining puzzle pieces.

"Cooper, it's your turn! Pick the next puzzle piece!"

Cooper, grinning playfully, waved his hand over the pieces, grabbed one, and gave it to the coach.

Turning the piece towards the Owls, Coach Ranger called out, "**Arrows-Out Attitude**. It's another key part of the mental game. In any sport, players play with either an Arrows-In or an Arrows-Out attitude."

Matt tilted his head, puzzled. "What's Arrows-In and Arrows-Out?"

Coach Ranger started explaining, "It's about the direction of your own energy. Arrows-In players feel like everything is against them and feel sorry for themselves. The energy arrows point back at them rather than out towards the game. They stay sad or mope and that's not a winning attitude."

The coach continued, "Arrows-In players feel like quitting when things don't go well. They're easy for other teams to beat. I'm guessing that during the Lizards game you felt Arrows-In. What does an Arrows-In attitude feel like?"

Noah put his hand up. "I felt defeated and drained of all my energy. It was like nothing was going right, so why even try? In that game I was totally Arrows-In."

"Exactly," the coach said. "So, if players go Arrows-In, are they giving their best on the next pitch? Does feeling Arrows-In help the team win?"

"No way!" they shouted in unison, shaking their heads.

"Let's look at the other attitude, Arrows-Out. Arrows-Out means you put all your energy into the game," Coach Ranger explained. "The energy arrows are pointing out from you. No feeling sorry for yourself. When things go wrong, you get tougher, keep trying, and give it your all every pitch. **Your goal is to always play with an Arrows-Out attitude on every pitch of every game.**"

Noah crossed his arms. "But sometimes, when I mess up, I get this sinking feeling right away. It's like I can't help going Arrows-In. It just happens."

Coach Ranger nodded. "That's true, Noah! When things get tough, almost all players slip into the Arrows-In attitude without realizing it."

Coach Ranger wrote in big, bold letters on the board: '**You Choose Your Attitude!**'

He then turned back to the team and, pointing to these words, said, "Here's a cool secret. You get to choose your attitude. You can choose to stay stuck in the mud with an Arrows-In attitude or choose to switch to playing Arrows-Out. Notice any Arrows-In feelings and change them right away. All of you have the power to do that. It's a power you didn't know you had, right?"

The team nodded knowingly.

Coach Wolf added, "Teams playing Arrows-Out are tough to beat. No matter what the score is, they don't quit. They keep coming after you. They fight to win every pitch like it's the first pitch of the game. There's no moping, pouting, or throwing temper tantrums. They choose to play Arrows-Out and have a winning attitude! It's a choice you can make, too."

"Trust me," Coach Wolf continued, "when you play Arrows-Out, everyone sees it. The fans, your coach, the other team, they all see and admire your fighting spirit. So, let's make Arrows-Out the only way the Owls play!"

Matt jumped up, his voice full of anticipation. "You got it! High energy and always Arrows-Out! We can do this, Owls!" His words pumped up everyone even more. "Let's go Owls!"

The team erupted into cheers, high fiving each other. They now had the first three pieces of the 'Win the Next Pitch' puzzle: **Keep Learning, Energy, and Arrows-Out Attitude.**

You're Up to Bat!

Jack says it's your turn to shine! Answering the questions helps you score runs. Answer one question? That's a single. Two? You've got a double. Three gets you a triple; four is a home run, and all five? You've hit a grand slam! Let's swing for the fences!

Chapter 4

1. What are some things you would write in your baseball notebook after playing?

2. Remember a time when you felt your energy was low during a game. Why do you think that happened?

3. How can you boost your energy during a game? How can your team help?

4. What do you think 'Arrows-in' and 'Arrows-Out' attitudes mean?

5. List the three puzzle pieces from this chapter. How can the lessons from this chapter help you and your team play better?

5

Training Your Brain Like a Puppy

Coach Ranger smiled widely, "Alright, team, let's find out what's next!"

Chase said excitedly, "I'll get it!" He picked up the next puzzle piece. "**Focus!**"

"Focus! How many times have you heard someone say that?" The coach cupped his hands around his mouth and raised his voice. "'You need to focus out there!' or 'You're losing your focus!'"

"So many times!" Jack said loudly as everyone else nodded.

"Imagine you're playing your favorite video game, and someone talks to you, or your phone buzzes. What happens?" the coach asked.

"You play worse," blurted Cooper.

"That's right," he said. "Baseball is the same. If you're distracted, you won't focus on the next pitch." Coach Ranger nodded.

Noah, listening carefully, spoke up, "Can we really stop thinking about other stuff?"

Coach Ranger tapped his head. "Yes, you can. Everyone can choose what they think about. Every day, many thoughts come into your head-some are good, and some are not. But guess what? You get to choose which ones to focus on and which to ignore. It's like being the boss of your thoughts, and that's a cool skill to learn!"

Noah's eyes lit up as he said, "I had no clue we could do that!"

The coach walked over to the whiteboard, picked up a marker, and with a big grin, began to draw a puppy.

"A puppy?" Matt whispered as the Owls, looking puzzled, leaned forward.

"Think of going for a walk with a puppy on a leash. You want him to walk straight down the sidewalk, but the puppy doesn't always cooperate. It might want to wander off to chase a squirrel or sniff a tree. You pull on the leash to get him back on track. You train him not to get distracted."

Coach Ranger then drew a kid walking a brain on a leash down a sidewalk, just like a puppy. "Training our brains is a lot like training a puppy. If you think about something other than winning the next pitch, pull your brain back on track. Pull that leash."

"You don't have to just let your brain go where it wants to go! Get back here!" The coach pretended to pull an imaginary leash. The boys laughed loudly, with a few of the Owls copying the coach's leash-pulling.

He continued with enthusiasm, "You have the power to control what you think about. It's your job to focus on the next pitch instead of any distractions. The more you practice using this power, the better you'll get at it."

Jack paused and looked up, thinking about the last game. *Against the Lizards, my mind drifted. I thought about my old friends, the rain, even Noah and his attitude. It just happened. Now, I know I can control what I think about.*

Coach Ranger asked, "A puppy gets distracted by a squirrel or a tree. What distracts us when we play baseball? I'll add them to our picture."

Nearly every hand quickly shot into the air. He pointed to Cooper, who was waving his arm back and forth.

"During our game against the Lizards, I focused too much on the weather," Cooper said. "The rain made everything muddy, and it distracted me for sure," he added, shaking his head.

The coach nodded. "That's a good one," he said. He added 'weather' to the drawing. Coach Ranger then asked, "Does worrying about the weather help you play better? Give you energy? Help your team? Help you focus on the next pitch?"

"No!" the boys answered.

The coach nodded. "That's right, it doesn't help. Both teams face the same weather and field conditions. When your brain wanders there, remember to pull it back!" Coach Ranger pretended to pull a leash again, and the Owls laughed. "What's another distraction?"

Jordan said, "Sometimes, I can't stop thinking about a mistake. My brain sticks on it, and I lose focus on the next pitch."

Coach Ranger scribbled 'mistakes' on his sidewalk picture. "Okay, let's talk about dwelling on past mistakes," he said. "Maybe it was a strikeout or a costly error. But you can't control or change what's already happened. Worrying takes away your focus on winning the next pitch. You can't do both at once. Baseball is played in the present. It's about this pitch, right here, right now. So, don't let thinking about past mistakes get you off track."

"Other distractions?" the coach asked, raising his eyebrows.

Noah's hand shot up. "The umpires. Last game, I worried about them too much. I watched a pitch go right down the middle for strike three. It was by me before I knew it. I guess my brain must have been wandering off the sidewalk," he said, pretending to lose the leash. The boys laughed.

Jack and Matt glanced at each other and nodded, remembering the at-bat Noah was talking about.

Coach Wolf jumped in, "That's right. What else distracted you, Noah?"

Noah squirmed a bit, then said, "I was also thinking too much about the other team and their pitcher. It made me forget to focus on the game."

Coach Ranger jotted 'umpires' and 'the other team' to the sides of the sidewalk in his drawing. He tapped the umpires and said, "Umpires might make mistakes, but we can't control that. Your job is to keep playing. If a call goes against you, just shake it off and focus on the next pitch. Complaining won't change anything."

"Now, thinking too much about the other team as a distraction." With a swift turn, he wrote on the board, **'Play the game first, not the other team.'**

Coach Ranger continued, "You're bound to play against better teams and faster pitchers. You'll be the underdog, sometimes. But there's an old saying in sports that I want you to remember. **'The best team doesn't always win the game. It's the team that plays the best that day.'** So just focus on playing the game of baseball. Compete, pitch by pitch. Worry about the final score when the game is over."

The coach then asked an interesting question. "What do all these distractions have in common?"

Matt thought for a moment, then said, "They're stuff we can't control!"

"Exactly!" Coach Ranger replied, spreading his arms. "The major distractions are things we can't control. Don't waste time thinking about them." He then wrote on the board **'Control what you can control!'**

Stepping back, Coach Ranger asked, "Who can tell us about this drawing?"

Jack went to the drawing and pointed. "It's like this: in a game, the things we can't control are like squirrels and trees to a puppy. They're very distracting. But we can decide what to focus on. We can control our thoughts instead of letting them automatically control us."

Clapping, Coach Ranger said, "You got it!"

"But how can we do it? My mind always wanders off, just like that puppy," Noah asked, looking puzzled.

Coach Ranger smiled, "Great question! Here's what you do!" He turned and wrote three steps on the whiteboard:

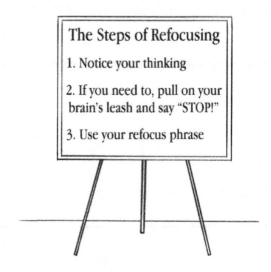

Turning to the team, he explained, "These are the three easy steps. First, pay attention to your thoughts. If you think about something other than the next pitch, do the next two steps."

Coach Ranger said, "For step two, pull the leash. Think 'STOP!' when your mind strays like you're stopping the puppy," he continued.

"Then, use your own refocus phrase. It's something you say to yourself and can be anything like 'Focus,' 'Next Pitch,' or 'Reset.' Pick one that brings your brain right back to what's most important, the next pitch. Back when I played, my refocus phrase was 'Get Back to Work.'"

Coach Wolf stepped forward. "Can anyone tell me how they'll use this in a game?"

Noah looked thoughtful. "I'll pay attention to what I'm thinking about. If my mind wanders, I'll pull it back to the next pitch. I'll say 'STOP' and use my refocus phrase. I like 'Reset' so I'll use that one. That'll get me ready for the next pitch in the game."

Coach Wolf grinned and patted Noah on the shoulder. "Perfect!" he said. "In your notebooks, write the refocus phrase you'll use. We'll practice these steps a lot, so they'll come naturally during games."

The Owls, impressed with this new skill, nodded in agreement, and jotted down their ideas. When they finished, Coach Ranger proudly lifted the **'Focus'** puzzle piece. He showed it to everyone, then carefully fit it into the growing puzzle.

The players watched intently, understanding the importance of this piece—not just in the puzzle, but in baseball and in life.

You're Up to Bat!

Jack says it's your turn to shine! Answering the questions helps you score runs. Answer one question? That's a single. Two? You've got a double. Three gets you a triple; four is a home run, and all five? You've hit a grand slam! Let's swing for the fences!

Chapter 5

1. Training your brain is like training a puppy. How is that true?

2. Why might thinking about the umpires or the other team distract you?

3. What does 'Control what you can control' mean in your own words?

4. What are Coach Ranger's three steps to refocus if you get distracted?

5. What 'refocus phrase' will you use to keep your mind on the next pitch?

6

Strike Out Doubt: Self-Talk Secrets

Like detectives on a mission, the Owls were exploring the secrets of baseball's mental game, finding one clue after another.

Coach Ranger, their mental game coach, stood in front of them with a big smile. "Owls, we're well on our way to building our 'Win the Next Pitch' puzzle!"

"Look," he said, pointing at the puzzle with four pieces already in place: **Keep Learning, Energy, Playing Arrows-**

Out, and **Focus**. "We have these four and just three more to go. Coach Wolf, your turn to pick!"

"Sure!" Coach Wolf bobbed his head, and the Owls moved aside as he leaned in over the table. He rubbed his chin and raised an eyebrow, pretending he was thinking hard. The boys laughed. He started to pick up each piece before choosing the middle one. With a playful grin, he handed it to Coach Ranger.

"**Positive Self-Talk**," announced Coach Ranger, showing the puzzle piece to the boys. "This one's a game-changer!"

"Self-what?" Drew asked, scratching his head.

"Self-talk is like a secret power in baseball," Coach Ranger explained. "What you say to yourself changes how you feel and your confidence. If you think, 'I can't do this' or 'I'm not good,' you start to believe it. It's like carrying a heavy backpack. Anyone ever felt that way?"

Drew's shoulders sank. "Yeah, like after our game with the Lizards. That voice kept telling me we're a bad team, and we'd probably lose every game. I felt really down."

"It happens to me when I'm batting. If I strike out the first time up, that voice inside my head says, 'Noah, you'll probably strike out this time, too.' It's like a thief sneaking in and stealing my confidence," Noah mumbled, his face turning red. "Does this happen to everyone?"

"Yes, Noah. Even the players you see on TV hear that voice, at least at first. But they've learned self-talk secrets that help them stay confident," the coach said, nodding. "I'll teach you the same self-talk tricks the pros use."

The Owls clustered around the whiteboard, eyes wide, as Coach Ranger wrote **'SELF-TALK TIPS'** in big, bold lettering.

1. Change negative self-talk to positive self-talk.

"Owls, here's the first trick: If you think something bad about yourself, don't believe it. Change it to something good. It's like switching the TV from a sad movie to a funny one," he said. "A lot of players don't realize they can change their thinking, but everyone can."

Cooper's hand shot up. "If I miss a ball and start thinking I'm a terrible catcher, I should change it right away. I should say something like, 'I'm a good catcher and I'll get the next one.'"

Coach Ranger tapped on the board. "That's right, Cooper!

"I tried that," Matt chimed in. "I missed an easy catch and thought, 'Matt, you're terrible.' But then, I switched it up. I told myself, 'You're a great centerfielder, Matt.' Instantly, I felt a boost of confidence. Guess what? The next fly ball? Caught it!"

Matt paused, his eyes lighting up. "I just thought of something. Changing your self-talk also helps you play with an Arrows-Out attitude. Instead of moping and pouting about the ball I missed, I focused all my energy outward towards winning that next pitch!"

Coach Ranger smiled, "Great point, Matt. Words like 'I'm terrible' or 'I can't' are Arrows-In words. Positive self-talk turns your arrows outward towards the game. That's playing Arrows-Out baseball."

Coach Wolf raised the Energy Meter and added, "Don't forget positive self-talk also helps keep the Energy Meter in the green."

Ah, I get it now, Jack thought. *All these tips work together. Each skill helps the others.*

"Switching from negative to positive self-talk is a big piece of our 'Win the Next Pitch' puzzle," Coach Ranger added. "So, catch those bad thoughts and change them to good ones."

Cooper said, "That's cool! I didn't know you can change your own thoughts. What other secrets are there about self-talk?" The team leaned in.

Coach Ranger looked at every player, taking his time. "Ah, good question. Here's another tip. I use it myself." With a twirl of his marker, he added another number to the board.

2. Remember, you CAN do tough things.

"Sometimes, when things get tough, my negative self-talk makes me doubt myself. It can be quite the troublemaker," he said.

"Thoughts like 'This is too hard' try to sneak in my head. But, like a catcher blocking a wild pitch, I stop them. I tell myself, 'Sure, it's hard, but I CAN do tough things.' Then I think of all the tough things I've done before. It's like getting a power-up in a video game. It boosts my energy and confidence. You boys can do the same thing."

The Owls exchanged glances as Coach Ranger went on. "Imagine you're at the plate, everyone is watching. You look the pitcher in the eyes, and he looks threatening. Instead of thinking, 'This guy's too tough,' or 'I just can't hit him,' tell yourself, 'Okay, he's tough, but I've hit tough pitchers before. I've done a lot of tough things before! I'm not scared!' Say it like you really mean it. Feel how that makes you more confident instead of worried."

"I'll start doing that when I pitch. If I think throwing a strike is too hard, I'll change my thinking. I'll say, 'It's hard, but I've done it lots of times.' This will really give me confidence on the next pitch." JJ grinned from ear to ear.

"Exactly right! Remembering something hard you've done before gives you an important confidence boost. I tell my team, 'If you've done something before, you can do it again.' It works for you hitters, too. Hitting with two strikes adds more pressure. But remembering you've gotten hits in that spot before boosts your confidence and keeps your nerves under control!"

Coach Ranger paced around the pavilion, tapping the marker against his hand. "Here's a cool thing," he said. "You can do this at school, too. Like when you're jittery about a test or speaking in front of the class. Just tell yourself that you've faced tough, scary stuff before, and you were successful. Every time you doubt, remind yourself, 'I can do tough things!' Let's shout that out together!"

"I can do tough things!" the Owls boomed out loud, exchanging high fives.

Jack whispered to Matt, "Like beating the Lizards!" Matt snickered, covering his mouth with his hand.

"Great job! Ready for the next tip?" he asked. The Owls nodded with anticipation.

Coach Ranger paced back to the board and glanced seriously at the boys before he slowly wrote another tip on the board.

3. Say what you WANT to have happen, not what you're AFRAID might happen.

"This tip is a game-changer, especially in pressure situations. It not only changes your feelings, but also the pictures you see in your mind," he said, tapping the board with the marker.

"Close your eyes, everyone. Imagine you're walking in the cafeteria, holding a tray with your favorite lunch. If you think, 'Don't drop this,' or 'Don't make a mess and embarrass yourself,' what picture pops up in your mind?"

"Splat! All over the place!" JJ shouted, spreading his arms out. The boys all laughed.

"Yes! When you think about what scares you, you often see it happening in your mind. It makes you more nervous and less confident," Coach Ranger said.

"Imagine you're batting with the bases loaded and two outs. If you say, 'Don't strike out,' how would that make you feel? What picture comes to mind?" he asked, looking around.

Noah's hand flew up. "That's easy because I've done that before. I pictured myself striking out and was way more nervous!"

"We've all done that, haven't we?" Matt said, looking around at his teammates. Every Owl nodded.

"Now think about this: instead of saying, 'Don't strike out,' you say 'Hit the ball hard!' What do you notice?" Coach Ranger looked at everyone.

"I'd see myself smashing the ball. I'd feel pretty powerful instead of nervous," Noah said, as he faked his swing.

"That's exactly it. When we talk about what we want to happen, it changes the video in our minds."

Crouching to the level of the team, Coach Ranger continued, "This tip is not only for baseball. It's good for other things too. If your dad plays golf and thinks, 'Don't hit the ball into the water,' what's he picturing? And what often ends up happening? Plop! Right into the water!" A ripple of giggles erupted from the Owls.

Still grinning, Jack thought, *I can't wait to tell my dad this tip. He's crazy about golf, and this could really help him. I've seen him hit the ball in the water before. He'll love it.*

JJ's hand went up. "Does this work for pitchers, too?"

"Sure! Imagine you have a 3-0 count on a batter. You need to throw the perfect pitch. Your self-talk kept saying, 'Don't walk him.' What would that be like?"

"That's easy!" JJ shook his head. "I just did that exact thing last game. Like Noah said, I'd get more stressed out. I'd see my next pitch being ball four, even before I ever threw it."

"That's right. Now think about that same 3-0 count, but this time, you tell yourself, 'Throw strikes,' or 'Hit your spot.' Wouldn't that change what you see and how you feel?"

"Yep! I'd be locked in and feel like I'm the boss out there. I'd see that pitch going right where I wanted it to go," JJ answered, flexing his wrist like he was throwing a fastball.

"So, Owls, right before each pitch, say what you want to happen, not what you're worried about. Everyone got that?" Coach Ranger asked.

"Got it!" answered the Owls in one voice.

"Any more tips on self-talk?" Jack asked.

"I have one more." Coach Ranger turned back to the board to write.

4. Treat yourself like you'd treat your best friend.

"Think about high fiving your best friend when he does something awesome. Feels good, right? When you do something great, treat yourself the same way! Use your thoughts to cheer yourself on! It builds confidence and reminds you that you're a good player."

"Now, think about if your friend just struck out. What would you tell him?"

Jack quickly said, "If Matt struck out, I'd tell him he's a good hitter and he'll get him next time."

"Hey, Jack!" Matt said jokingly. "Didn't have to call me out." The boys laughed along with their star player.

"I'd say the same," Noah said above the laughter, raising his eyebrows and nodding.

"Why would you say that to Matt?" Coach Ranger asked, motioning to everyone to quiet down.

"I want to keep him confident. That helps him play better in the game," Jack said, nodding.

"So, you wouldn't tell Matt, 'You're awful!' or 'You can't hit!' or 'You should just stop playing baseball!'" Coach Ranger said.

The Owls shook their heads and laughed at such a strange idea.

"You wouldn't, but I bet you've said mean things like that to yourself after you struck out or made an error," the coach said.

The Owls ducked their heads, murmuring about their experiences with bad self-talk.

"Remember, your words are powerful. They can boost you up or drag you down. Sometimes we're too hard on ourselves. When that happens, it's like the air goes out of a balloon. We feel sad and less confident. It doesn't help us win the next pitch."

Coach Ranger sat on the table facing the team. "Self-talk is a huge part of the mental game puzzle. You always have the power to choose what you say to yourself. Be like a detective with your thoughts, especially when you mess up. Watch carefully what you say and change the negative self-talk to positive self-talk."

He grabbed a baseball, playfully threw it up, caught it, then said, "Just like you practice your batting and catching, practice positive self-talk. Use these tips, like the pros do, and you'll play better baseball."

He showed the **Positive Self-Talk** puzzle piece and fit it into the almost finished puzzle. Learning positive self-talk wasn't just making the Owls better at baseball. It was teaching them how to be successful in everything they do.

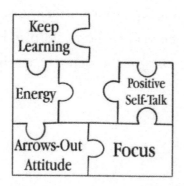

You're Up to Bat!

Jack says it's your turn to shine! Answering the questions helps you score runs. Answer one question? That's a single. Two? You've got a double. Three gets you a triple; four is a home run, and all five? You've hit a grand slam! Let's swing for the fences!

Chapter 6

1. What's a positive thing you can say to yourself if you feel nervous during a game?

2. Make a list of things you say to your friend after he strikes out. Now, make a list of things you've said to yourself after a strikeout. Look at both lists. What did you notice?

3. Why is it important to say what you want to happen, instead of what you're afraid might happen? What changes in your mind when you do this? Write down a game situation where this will be very helpful!

4. How does 'I can do tough things' help you in sports, school, and other areas?

5. List Coach Ranger's four self-talk tips. Jack was going to teach these tips to his dad so he could play better golf. Help a teammate, parent, or your coach by teaching them Coach Ranger's tips.

7

Controlling Emotions:
Resetting with the 3 Ts

The Owls huddled around Coach Ranger, all looking excited.

Jack inched even closer, so close that his cap brushed against Matt's sandy hair. He whispered, his eyes bright, "What's next?"

Matt grinned, eyeing the puzzle pieces left on the table. "No clue, but they've been awesome so far."

Coach Ranger, shooting them a mischievous grin, said, "Alright, Owls, who's next? JJ, your turn!"

JJ, his long, curly hair peeking out from under his cap, eagerly snatched the nearest puzzle piece.

"Control Your Emotions," JJ declared, excitement in his voice. He shot Noah a playful look, and he grinned back, his cheeks turning a little red.

Coach Ranger put up his finger. "Controlling your emotions is a big deal. It can totally change how you play. What are some feelings you have when you play baseball?"

"Happiness," Jack said, his face lit up.

Matt bounced a bit. "Excitement," he shared. "I'm always excited to start a new game or play in a big tournament."

Cooper shuffled his feet, looking down, then murmured, "Maybe sadness, like when we're losing, or I mess up."

"Anxiety." Chase, the team's jokester, grinned. "You know, getting super nervous." Chase, pretending his legs were shaking, set off a wave of laughter among the boys.

Noah scrunched his eyebrows. "Anger and frustration. That's what bugs me, like when I strike out."

Jack grinned, remembering Noah's many tantrums, and glanced at Matt, who smiled back and whispered, "Yeah, we've seen that before."

The coach nodded. "Good job, Owls! Feeling happy or excited makes you play better. But being nervous or angry does not. When you're too nervous or angry, it can be tough to focus on the most important thing in baseball. And what's that?" He looked at the team, his voice filled with anticipation.

"The next pitch!" the Owls shouted together.

"Exactly!" exclaimed the coach. He hustled to the whiteboard and scribbled in bold letters, **'You have to control your emotions before you can control how you play.'**

"Even the pro players get anxious or angry at times. The secret is knowing how to deal with those tough feelings. I've got some simple yet powerful techniques to teach you, like deep breathing and the 3 Ts."

Every boy knew what it was like to feel nervous or mad during a game. They leaned in, ready to hear something big.

Coach Ranger put the marker down and rubbed his hands together. He said, "Let's start with feeling nervous. It's normal to feel anxious sometimes. Even the big-league players get jittery, especially in big games. A bit of nervousness is okay. But being super nervous? That's when playing gets tough. You might feel your heart racing, your body tightening up, and your breathing speed up. And your head? Full of thoughts. Has that happened to any of you?"

The Owls glanced at each other, nodding. Chase shook his legs a bit and grinned.

"Chase, how's your breathing?"

Chase smiled widely. "I guess I'm a pro at it. I do it every day!"

The boys all laughed.

Coach Ranger chuckled. "True, but let's learn a special way to breathe when you're nervous. It's called deep breathing. It's such a great skill that even the pros do it! Deep breathing calms you down fast. It slows everything down in your body so you can think clearer and focus on the next pitch."

The coach said, "Let's try something fun. Stand up and breathe like you're nervous. You know, fast and shallow. Ready? Go!" The boys giggled and panted.

After a bit, he said, "Okay, stop! How did you feel? Relaxed?" He looked at them, curious to hear their thoughts.

"No way! I felt all jumpy and my muscles got tight. I was a bit scared too," Drew said, appearing surprised.

"Now, for deep breathing. Close your eyes. Slowly breathe in through your nose and count to four. Picture the air going down into your belly, making it puff out."

The boys did just that. "Now, hold your breath for a second or two. Then, breathe out through your mouth like you're blowing out candles. Picture the worries flying away with that breath. Let your shoulders relax. Let's practice this a few more times."

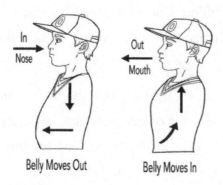

Belly Moves Out   Belly Moves In

The coach instructed, "Act like you're smelling a flower, then blowing out candles on your birthday cake."

"When you're done, stop and notice how you feel. Is your heart beating slower? Are you more relaxed?" he asked, glancing around.

"I am for sure!" Noah said with a nod.

"Me too," said another Owl.

"I almost fell asleep," Chase joked. Jack gave him a friendly shove. The other Owls couldn't help but smile.

Coach Ranger grinned. "See? It works! It's like you're telling your body everything is okay. Deep breathing is like a superpower. Use it anytime you're feeling anxious, no matter where you are."

"It works anywhere?" Noah asked, his eyes wide with wonder.

"Yep! I even did it at the dentist last week. I was nervous waiting to get a filling. But a few deep breaths calmed me down fast." The coach playfully opened his mouth and pointed to a back tooth.

"I did deep breathing at a sports dinner," Coach Wolf added. "I had to speak in front of everyone and was super nervous. So, before my speech, I took some nice deep breaths, and I felt a lot better. It works great anytime, anywhere."

I'll use this at school before the big test coming up next week, Jack thought as he took another deep breath and let it out.

The whole team started practicing deep breathing, their faces relaxing.

Coach Wolf smiled. "Like Coach Ranger said, all pro athletes use deep breathing to relax. Pay attention, and you'll see baseball players do this before pitches and basketball players before shooting free throws. Now, you have their secret on how to stop feeling so nervous!"

Coach Ranger clapped. "Alright! Let's learn a great way to deal with being mad or frustrated."

He tossed a baseball into the air and caught it. "Baseball can be tough. We try to be perfect, but nobody is, not even the pros. They're the best players in the world, but sometimes they still strike out, miss grounders, and walk batters. They get upset when they make mistakes, just like us. But they've learned how to get over those feelings quickly before the next pitch. I'll show you how."

The coach wrote in big letters on the whiteboard for everyone to see:

Coach Ranger smiled. "Imagine this: you're playing outside, and suddenly, it starts to rain. What do you do? You don't just stand there pouting because it's raining. You run and grab your raincoat or an umbrella, right? Mistakes in baseball are like unexpected rain. They're going to happen. So, we need a plan to deal with them, like our raincoat keeps us from getting soaked."

He continued, "In baseball, making an error or striking out is like getting hit by surprise raindrops. We don't like making mistakes, but mistakes are part of the game. The important thing, just like when it rains, is you don't just sit there. You **do something** to shake it off and get ready for the next pitch. That **something** is using a reset to stop from feeling bad. Feeling mad or sorry for yourself doesn't help anyone, especially the team."

"Let me ask you this," Coach Ranger said, looking at everyone. "If players stay pouting, are they going to be ready for the next pitch? "

"Nope! I've been there!" Noah said.

"Right, and what happens then?" he asked.

"They'll miss the next one," JJ said, nodding.

"Yes, if we don't reset, mistakes keep happening," the coach explained. "It's because our minds can't focus on the last play and the next play at the same time."

"So, I reset after a mistake. But what's a reset?" JJ asked, leaning in.

Jack gave Matt a quick glance, as they both already knew about resetting.

"What do you guys do when your video game messes up?" Coach Ranger asked, walking back and forth.

"I hit the reset button. It starts it all over again, like it's brand new," Cooper said confidently.

"Pressing reset makes things new, like a fresh start. Think of each baseball pitch as a new game. Messed up? It's okay. Just press your reset using a cool trick called the 3 Ts," Coach Ranger explained.

"These are three steps of the 3 Ts for resetting." Coach Ranger said, holding up three fingers. "First, **'Take deep breaths.'** Like we practiced. They help you calm down when you're frustrated. They slow your body and mind down, getting you back in control. Take as many deep breaths as you need." He took a big, slow breath.

Step 1. Take a Deep Breath

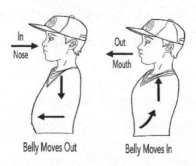

Belly Moves Out   Belly Moves In

"The second T, is to **'Throw away the mistake.'** Do something physical to get rid of it, like you are throwing it in the trash. If you're in the field, grab some dirt, squeeze it, and toss it away. Hitters can sweep the batter's box with their foot. When you do this, tell yourself the mistake is gone for good. Can't change it, so let it go, and focus on the next pitch."

Step 2. Throw away the mistake

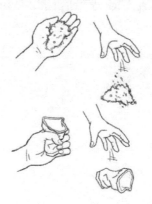

"What about pitchers? Can pitchers do something like that?" JJ asked.

"Sure, JJ!" the coach answered. "Pitchers can toss dirt, squeeze the rosin bag, wipe their foot on the rubber, or swipe your glove on your leg. Anything that works for you to get rid of that last pitch. You're now starting fresh. You're ready for the next pitch."

Noah piped up, holding an imaginary bat, "And us hitters, Coach? What can we do after a bad at-bat?"

"You hitters? You need a reset too," the coach assured the group. "After a tough at-bat, maybe crush a water cup like you're squashing your mistake. Toss it in the trash can. That bad at-bat? Gone! Reset and get ready to get a hit the next time you're up."

"The last T," Coach Ranger said, "is to **'Tell yourself something positive.'** After making a mistake, don't be too hard on yourself. There's no time for that. You must quickly get ready for the next pitch."

Step 3. Tell yourself positive things

No problem, I'll rip it the next time up!

I'm a good player!

Next time, I'll make a great play!

He continued, "Negative self-talk just makes you feel worse and hurts your chances of making the next play. Instead, remind yourself you're a good player and you'll get the next one. Every pitch is a new opportunity, so reset and be ready."

"Let's do this," the coach said. "Write the throwaway behaviors and positive self-talk you'll use after a mistake. Make up different ones for the field and batting. You'll try them out in practice to see what works best."

The boys started writing their thoughts in their new notebooks.

"What will you use?" Matt asked Jack quietly.

"I'll use what you showed me earlier this season," Jack told Matt. "If I make an error, I'll grab some dirt and toss it away. After a bad at-bat, I'll squash the water cup. They worked great last game."

"Those are good! Just practice the 3 Ts and always make sure once you throw the mistake away, you never think about it again. It's on to the next pitch," Matt reminded Jack.

Soon, the Owls had finished writing and shared their ideas with the coaches.

Coach Wolf said, "Great ideas, Owls. From now on, we'll use the 3 Ts for resets in practice. We'll do it every time things don't go well. Our goal is to become pros at letting go of mistakes."

Coach Ranger added, "Using the 3 Ts is a much better way to handle anger and frustration than moping, pouting, or throwing a tantrum. Those things just make you look bad to everyone. They also won't give you the best chance of success on the next pitch."

Smiling, Coach Ranger showed them the puzzle piece again. "So, Owls, to play our best, **we need to control our emotions**. Can anyone review what we learned?"

Jack stood confidently, with the eyes of his teammates on him. "Guys, we've learned a lot about how to handle our feelings today. For nerves, we take our deep breaths, like smelling flowers and blowing out candles. It calms us anytime, anywhere."

Then he said, "For anger from mistakes, remember, everyone messes up. Reset with the 3 Ts: Breathe, throw the mistake away, and say something good to yourself. It's like restarting a video game. Every pitch gives us a new chance to do something great. No moping, no pouting, no tantrums!"

Coach Ranger and Coach Wolf, looking happy, nodded. Jack's review was right on target. Now, the team knew how to handle tough feelings like worry and anger. By using deep breathing and the 3 Ts, they could keep their minds on winning the next pitch!

You're Up to Bat!

Jack says it's your turn to shine! Answering the questions helps you score runs. Answer one question? That's a single. Two? You've got a double. Three gets you a triple; four is a home run, and all five? You've hit a grand slam! Let's swing for the fences!

Chapter 7

1. What is a "reset"? How does it help?

2. Try the deep breathing right now. Make sure you are doing it exactly right, nice, and slow. Describe how it feels.

3. Where else will you use deep breathing besides baseball?

4. Can you explain the 3 Ts in your own words?

5. Look for players using deep breathing before a pitch in games or videos. What did you notice?

The Final Puzzle Piece:
Stop Thinking and Start Hitting!

Coach Ranger waved the Owls closer to the table. "Guess what team? It's time for the last piece of our mental game puzzle." He pointed to their progress so far.

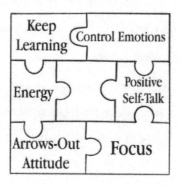

"Jack, are you ready to flip over the last piece?"

Jack's face brightened. He flipped it over and announced, "'**Pre-Pitch Routines**.' Matt taught this to me, and it works great," he said, holding the piece for all to see. "Can I explain it?" he asked the coaches, smiling confidently.

"Absolutely, go ahead!" Coach Wolf encouraged. "Coach Ranger and I are here to help."

Picking up the coach's bat, Jack took a few easy swings. "Matt shared this hitting secret earlier this season. And guess what? It really works! It's a special pre-pitch routine like college and pro players use."

"What's a pre-pitch routine exactly?" asked Noah.

Jack propped the bat against the table. "It's what you do before each pitch. Maybe you swing a certain number of times, step into the batter's box in a special way, tap the plate, or wave your bat around. It's your own habit. Everyone's routine is different."

Cooper added, "I always take two practice swings and then touch every corner of the plate. It helps me feel calm, kind of like a good luck charm, I guess."

"Yep, that's right," Jack said, nodding. "Routines make us feel ready and calm. It's like we've been here before. We all use them. They're also a bit like superstitions too, making us think doing the same thing brings good luck."

Jack's eyes widened like he had a secret to share. "I have a new pre-pitch routine that's a game-changer. It's even better than what you're doing now. This routine keeps you from thinking too much when you are batting. You see, players can't think and hit at the same time. Your brain has to react fast, and thinking slows your reaction time." He took a pretend swing.

Noah looked amazed. "Wow, I think too much sometimes. My mind goes so fast I can't focus. Everything seems to speed up, and I feel all jittery. When that happens, the pitch is by me before I know it."

"We've all been there, especially in big games," Jack said. His teammates nodded.

Jack leaned closer with a serious look. "Your mind should be empty right before each pitch. The best hitters aren't thinking. They just react. See the ball, hit the ball. The routine I'm going to show you helps you do just that."

Cooper paused, a light bulb going off in his head. "It's like when I'm playing video games. I hear nothing else. I don't even talk to myself. I'm totally focused, just reacting to what's happening in the game."

"Right," Jack agreed. "We need that same kind of focus when we bat. No thinking, just reacting."

Noah tilted his head, his eyebrows furrowing, and asked, "But how do we do that?"

Jack grinned as he explained, "Here are four simple steps for an amazing pre-pitch routine. This routine is easy to learn, and with practice, you'll do it without even thinking. Wanna try it?"

"You bet!" the Owls shouted, all eager to become better hitters.

"Alright, go grab your bats and let's go to the cages," Coach Wolf called out. The Owls rushed to their bags, grabbing their bats like knights ready for battle. With bats ready, they gathered at the batting cages.

Jack began and stepped forward as if approaching the plate. "Let me show you the four steps to the perfect pre-pitch routine."

"First, before stepping into the batter's box, check with the third-base coach for your signs. It's alright to think here—about the game situation, what pitch you want, and what the coach wants you to do. This is the only time you will do any thinking."

Step 1. Look at Coach

Jack went on. "The next three steps are super important. We all get nervous sometimes when we're batting, right? So, for step two, take a deep breath, just like Coach Ranger showed us. This breath helps calm your body and quiets your mind right before each pitch."

Step 2. Take a Deep Breath

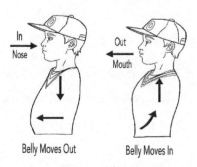

Belly Moves Out   Belly Moves In

Chase's eyes widened. "I saw you and Matt doing that breathing thing last game!"

Matt smiled and nodded. "I do that before every pitch." He took a slow, deep breath in, then out.

Jack added, "If you're still feeling nervous, take a few more breaths. Sometimes, I take two or three. Remember, breathe slowly—no need to rush."

Coach Wolf clapped. "Let's practice these first two steps now." The Owls pretended they were coming to bat. They glanced at their make-believe coach and took deep breaths.

Coach Ranger scanned the team, smiling. "Awesome job! How does everyone feel now?"

Noah spoke up, his voice calm. "I feel much more relaxed now. My mind isn't racing like before."

"Good!" Coach Wolf said before turning to Jack. "Okay, Jack, what's next? The third step?"

Jack leaned closer, whispering like he was sharing a secret. "Step three is super important, maybe the most important. It's an easy way to stop all your thinking. Remember, thinking hurts your concentration on the pitch."

Jack pointed to his bat. "Now, check this out. Pick a small spot on your bat. This is your personal 'focus point.' It's like a magic switch that turns off all those racing thoughts."

Step 3. Study Focus Point

He pointed to a small scratch on his bat. "It can be a scuff, a letter, or a tiny design—anything small that catches your eye. Look at it closely, as if you're seeing it for the first time. Notice every little detail. When you do this, nothing else exists—just you and that spot. Do this right and all your thoughts disappear. Your brain is quiet and now ready to react to the pitch."

Matt, eager, jumped in. "Remember, practice makes perfect. Soon, you'll be able to switch off your thoughts quicker than turning off a light. No more getting distracted, not by the crowd, not by the pitcher."

He swung in slow motion. "It's just you and the ball—bam!"

Jack's eyes lit up as he went on, "Now for the last step. Move your eyes from the focus point on your bat to the pitcher's release point. The release point is that area beside the pitcher's head where the pitcher lets the ball go. I pretend it's like a video game, waiting for the ball to pop out from there. Going from your focus point directly to the release point helps you see the ball better and react quicker."

Step 4. Look Only at the Release Point

Chase looked curious. "So, I look at the release point? I don't look at the pitcher's face or anywhere else?"

"Nope!" Jack confirmed. "Looking anywhere else distracts you. Imagine your eyes are a laser moving from the spot on your bat to the release point. You'll track the pitch much better. Not a strike? Let it go. A strike? Smash it!"

The players were eager to try out their new routine. The coaches watched closely, making sure everyone took their time with each step. As practice went on, the Owls started hitting better than ever. With every swing, their confidence soared.

Jack nudged Matt, smiling proudly. "Look at them! They're ripping a lot of line drives."

Matt grinned back. "You explained it perfectly. We both know this routine works great."

"It's a game-changer. I'm a much tougher hitter now," Jack said, nodding to Matt.

As they finished the hitting drills, Coach Wolf gathered the team. "Awesome work today! This pre-pitch routine is your secret to stop thinking and just focus on the pitch. Keep practicing it. Use it every pitch. You'll notice a big improvement in your hitting."

With a wide smile, Coach Ranger suggested, "Let's head back to the pavilion, team, and put this final piece into our puzzle."

The team, buzzing with excitement over their new skills, rushed over to the big table. They gathered around as Coach Ranger placed the **'Pre-Pitch Routine'** piece into the puzzle. Pointing to the completed puzzle, he announced, "Here they are! Seven powerful mental game skills that, with practice, will make you all fantastic baseball players."

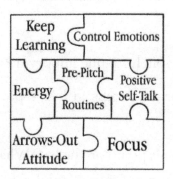

Cooper, nodding excitedly, exclaimed, "I can't wait to try everything we learned!"

Coach Wolf, just as enthusiastic as his team, announced, "You'll have your chance soon. We're not in a tournament this weekend, so Coach Ranger and I decided it'll be the Owls and the Lizards this Saturday. Let's meet at one o'clock at Shally Field."

The Owls cheered and whooped, and Coach Wolf laughed as he looked around at his young team. What began as just another practice day turned into something remarkable. Armed with valuable mental skills, the boys left the field overflowing with newfound confidence. Now, instead of fearing the Lizards, the Owls couldn't wait to play them on Saturday.

You're Up to Bat!

Jack says it's your turn to shine! Answering the questions helps you score runs. Answer one question? That's a single. Two? You've got a double. Three gets you a triple; four is a home run, and all five? You've hit a grand slam! Let's swing for the fences!

Chapter 8

1. Why is a pre-pitch routine important?

2. What are the four steps in Jack's pre-pitch routine? Do you like them?

3. What is a 'focus point' on the bat? What does it do to your brain? Why is it important for your mind to be empty before each pitch?

4. How could using Jack's routine change your game? Try it out in the batting cages.

5. Write the seven mental game skills in the puzzle . Which is your favorite?

9

It's the Owls vs. the Lizards:
The Rematch of the Year!

The sun smiled down on Shally Field, making everything bright. It was a big day. The Oak Grove Owls were up against their rivals, the L-Burg Lizards. A gentle breeze played in the air, carrying the fresh scent of newly cut grass. The field was alive with excitement. Players were everywhere, stretching like cats in the sun, tossing baseballs back and forth, and practicing their swings. It was a perfect day to play baseball.

As Jack walked past the concession stand, he heard the *pop-pop-pop* of popcorn. The air was thick with the smell of salt and butter. He quickly dodged a boy carrying a soda and a hotdog that was spilling over with ketchup. Jack reached into his pocket and pulled out a piece of gum. He chomped on it quickly, then blew a bubble so big it nearly covered his face. Laughing, he kept walking to the dugout, ready for the game.

He stepped onto the field, pausing for a moment to take it all in. Coach Wolf was in the dugout scribbling down the lineup. In the outfield, Jordan and a few other players tossed the ball back and forth, their laughter floating in the air. Danny was swinging his shiny new two-toned black bat near the backstop. Cooper, holding his catcher's mask under his arm, listened intently to JJ, the team's star pitcher, sharing some last-minute strategies.

"Are we ready to show those Lizards what we've got?" Matt asked, tossing a ball to Jack, who caught it with ease.

"Totally," Jack said, flashing his friend a toothy smile.

"Were those mental game lessons cool or what?" Matt asked as he tightened his shoelaces.

Jack nodded, feeling confident. "Oh yeah. I learned so much and can't wait to try them out today. It'll be fun."

Jack continued, "My dad and I went to the batting cages and worked on the pre-pitch routine. And I've filled up that notebook Coach Wolf gave us with everything we learned about the mental game." Jack patted his bat bag. "I'm keeping that thing right in here, in case I need a tip or two."

"Smart thinking! Mine's full and I brought it too. How about we head out to the outfield and throw?" Matt suggested, already heading in that direction.

Just then, a loud voice came from across the field. "Hey, Jack!" It was Alex. Even from far away, Jack could see his big smile.

"Good luck today!" Alex yelled over, cupping his hand and glove around his mouth so he could be heard.

Jack's face stretched with a wide smile. "Thanks! You too, Alex!" he shouted back, his hand pointing at the Lizards' shortstop.

On his way to the outfield, Jack spotted Noah, the Owls backup pitcher, in the bullpen. He was working on his pitches. The lefty scrunched his eyebrows together, scowling after each throw.

"Not again," Noah muttered, kicking the dirt. His change-up, usually his go-to pitch, was giving him trouble today. It was out of the strike zone or not changing speed enough. Noah bit his lip, looking down.

Jack stopped his jog and walked closer to watch the struggling pitcher. He wanted to help, but didn't know how.

Just then, Preston Jones, the Lizards' star pitcher and Jack's friend, ran up and greeted him. "Hey, Jack! You pumped for the game today?" Preston asked as he put his arm around Jack's shoulder.

"Always ready! It's going to be a blast," Jack said, as he kept glancing at Noah.

Preston followed Jack's gaze to Noah and noticed the pitcher's struggles. "Having trouble with the change-up, huh?" Preston asked with genuine curiosity.

"Yeah," Jack admitted. "It's usually one of his best pitches. He just can't seem to get it right today."

Preston watched Noah throw a few more pitches, then said, "I see something that might help. Mind if I give him a couple of tips? The change-up can be tricky."

Jack's eyes widened, and he smiled. "That would be awesome, Preston. Thanks!"

They walked over to Noah, who looked up, unsure. "Hey, Noah, want me to show you a few things about the change-up? I've had my share of battles with it too," Preston offered, his tone friendly, without a hint of rivalry.

Noah paused and glanced at Preston's Lizard uniform, then nodded. He slowly handed Preston the baseball.

Preston got right into it. He showed Noah a little different grip and made a throwing motion with his arm. "Try to keep your arm speed the same as your fastball and check your grip," Preston explained.

Noah took Preston's advice and gave it another try. This time, his change-up floated in, deceptive and precise. A grin broke out on Noah's face.

"Hey, it worked! Thanks, Preston, that's awesome!" Noah said, now looking him in the eyes.

"No problem. Glad I could help! Good luck today," Preston said with a nod before jogging across the outfield to his team.

Noah turned to Jack, still smiling. "That was cool of him to give me those tips. I feel like I got it now." His confidence grew as he continued to practice his pitches. Each change-up was better than the last.

Jack smiled back and nodded before sprinting into the outfield to warm up with Matt. *It's good to see Noah being nicer to me. Maybe he's also seeing that the Lizards aren't bad guys after all.*

Soon, Coach Wolf, looking serious, gathered the team in the dugout. "Are you ready to play? Let's use what you've learned about the mental game. The next pitch is always the most important one of the game. Play the game pitch by pitch!"

Coach Wolf pointed to the Energy Meter hanging in the dugout. "Let's make sure this meter stays green! And let's see those Arrow-Out Attitudes, no matter what happens!"

Matt added, "Like coach said, just focus on winning each new pitch. We're a good team. Let's show the Lizards what we're made of!"

Jack stepped up. "Owls on three!"

"One, two, three, OWLS!" they shouted, their powerful voices spilling into the stands.

Charged with excitement, the Owls sprinted onto the field. Full of chatter, their infield practice was perfect. JJ's warm-up pitches hit their mark. Noah was throwing the ball to every infielder, and they had no trouble with the ground balls. In the outfield, Matt's long toss with Jason was further than ever. Cooper jogged to the mound and offered some last-second advice to JJ, whose hair bounced as he nodded. He hustled back behind the plate.

"Let's play ball!" shouted the umpire.

The game began with a sharp strike from JJ. The Owls cheered from the field.

We've got this. It's time to show off what we've learned! Jack thought, smacking his fist into his glove.

For the next few hours, Shally Field became their whole world. Both teams were determined to give it everything they had—every pitch, swing, and catch.

The game was tense, with neither team scoring in the first inning. JJ sent three Lizards back to the dugout with two strikeouts and an easy pop-up. In the bottom of the inning, it was Preston's turn to shine. The Lizards' ace struck out Drew, Chase, and Cooper, with no one even fouling off a pitch. With each strikeout, the Owls' spirits sank.

The Owls shuffled onto the field for the top of the second. Their shoulders slumped, having witnessed Preston's domination. Just like last season, it seemed impossible to score against the Lizards' star pitcher.

"Owls! Owls! Let's go!" Coach Wolf shouted as he pointed to the Energy Meter, with its arrow as far into the red as it could go.

The Owls knew the coach was right. Low energy would not win this game. They picked up their hustle. Their infield practice was crisp, and the Owls' chatter returned. Once again, they were ready to play.

JJ cruised through another inning. He got the Lizards' clean-up hitter to fly out to centerfield. Ground ball outs to Danny at shortstop and Drew at second base took care of the next two batters.

"Way to throw strikes, JJ!" Jack said, high fiving him as they jogged off the field.

"Thanks. Our awesome defense makes my job easier," JJ said, nodding proudly.

The Owls' best hitter, Matt, was leading off the bottom of the second inning. Noah, Jack, and Danny would follow. During warm-ups, Preston threw the ball so hard that each pitch smacked into the mitt with a sound as loud as thunder. After the final warm-up throw, the catcher yanked off his mitt and shook his left hand, trying to get rid of the sting of Preston's fastballs.

In the dugout, Noah gripped his bat tightly, his knuckles turning white. He looked at Jack with wide eyes, "Wow, he throws hard." Flashbacks from last year danced in his head—

Preston had struck him out five out of five times. "I just can't hit this guy," Noah muttered. "He's going to strike me out again."

Hearing Noah's negative self-talk, Jack looked at the doubting hitter. "Hey, Noah, remember how we talked about thinking positive? You gotta believe you can hit him," he said, trying to boost his friend's confidence.

"Don't say 'You can't.' Say, 'I *can* hit this pitcher. I'm an awesome hitter.' Just do your routine and take it one pitch at a time. Each pitch is a new battle. You can do it!" Jack beamed with confidence.

Taking a deep, calming breath, Noah repeated Jack's words. Jack watched as Noah took a few more deep breaths as he walked to the on-deck circle. There, Noah swung with power and ease. After Matt flew out to center field for the first out, it was Noah's turn to hit.

He looks confident. Noah's doing exactly what we talked about, Jack thought as he watched Noah march to home plate.

Noah carefully did his pre-pitch routine and stood ready in the batter's box, his jaw clenched in determination, not fear. Preston wound up and unleashed a fastball. Noah took an aggressive swing. The ball zipped past him.

Strike one.

Noah didn't let it rattle him. He went through the steps of his pre-pitch routine. It was a glance at his coach, a deep breath, the focus point, and eyes directly out to the release point.

Preston, with a sly grin, threw a changeup next. Noah, expecting another fastball, was fooled, and swung too early, missing the ball completely.

Strike two.

Down two strikes, Noah didn't look worried.

"Look at that. Noah's keeping his cool. That's a really good sign," Matt whispered to Cooper, both watching his every move.

Noah stepped out of the box. Once again, he did the same steps of his pre-pitch routine. Preston threw another fastball, thinking he could blow it by him. But this time, Noah was ready. He swung with perfect timing. The crack of the bat echoed through the field as the ball soared deep to centerfield before hitting the top of the fence.

Noah bolted past first base and skidded to a stop at second. His heart pounded with joy and pride. He had done it—he finally got a hit off Preston, and not just any hit, but a double!

As he stood on second base trying to catch his breath, Alex, the Lizards shortstop, jogged over and tapped him on the leg with his glove. "Nice hit. I thought that was going to be outta here!"

"Thanks!" Noah wheezed, a smile filling his face.

Preston walked behind the pitcher's mound. "Great hit, Noah. I guess I should've thrown you another changeup," he said with a slight grin.

Noah, feeling a mix of relief and happiness, grinned back. "Thanks, Preston. Maybe next time," he replied, adjusting his helmet with both hands.

Back in the dugout, Noah's teammates were all smiles with high fives, celebrating his success. Jack flashed Noah a thumbs-up as he walked up to bat, his confidence high. With a runner on second, he knew a base hit would give the Owls the lead.

Jack glanced down at Coach Wolf, coaching third base. "Hit your pitch, Jack! Right hitter, right time!" the coach yelled, clapping loudly.

Jack took his deep breath, zeroed in on his focus point, and his eyes went right to Preston's release point.

Preston, with renewed determination, fired his best fastball of the day. Jack swung and missed. The ball zipped by him before he knew it.

Strike one.

"A little quicker! You can get him, Jack," Matt called from the dugout.

"Each pitch is a new chance," Jack reminded himself. *Look for the change-up,* he thought.

Jack did his pre-pitch routine and dug into the batter's box. Preston reached back and threw another blazing fastball. Expecting a change-up, Jack froze. The pitch was right down the middle.

"Steeerike two," the umpire shouted, his right arm punching the air.

A wave of panic came over Jack. His thoughts raced. *Wow, two strikes. I'm in trouble. Don't strike out. Whatever you do, don't strike out!* Jack's heart pounded and his breath quickened as images of him striking out filled his mind.

Above the growing crowd noise, Jack heard Coach Wolf shout, "You're okay! It just takes one!"

Jack knew he was right. Baseball is all about taking it pitch by pitch. *Just win the next pitch,* he thought.

Jack closed his eyes, took a few deep breaths, and remembered Coach Ranger's advice. "Say what you *want* to have happen, not what you're *afraid of,*" he whispered.

With an extra deep breath, he thought, *Hit the ball hard. Hit the ball hard.* The picture of him striking out was gone, replaced by a video of the ball rocketing off his bat.

A wave of calm washed over him, and Jack went through his routine once more. His mind was quiet as he looked out at Preston's release point. It was going to be the baseball coming out of the hand and nothing else.

Preston stared at his catcher, shook off a sign, and glanced at Noah leading off second. He sent the next pitch, a blazing fastball, screaming towards home plate. Jack swung.

Crack!

Jack felt the bat vibrate in his hands and saw the line drive zip past a ducking Preston and into centerfield. Jack bolted to first base, his helmet bouncing with each step, and his heart pounding like a drum.

I did it! I did it! he thought as he rounded first base and then hustled back to the bag safely.

Noah dashed home from second, putting the Owls ahead 1-0.

"Way to go, Jack! Nice hit!" Noah's voice cut through the cheers. Jack pumped his fist, his cheeks pulled tightly in a huge smile. He caught sight of his parents in the stands, who were now jumping and waving.

"Nice hit, Jack!" his dad shouted.

"Way to go! I knew you could do it!" his mother added, jumping up and down.

Jack's eyes focused on Preston, who remained calm. He took a few deep breaths, picked up the rosin bag, tossed it down, and whispered something to himself.

He's doing the 3 Ts, Jack thought.

The Lizards' pitcher's reset worked. He threw perfect pitches to the next two batters and struck out Danny and JJ to end the inning.

10

Trouble for the Owls?

Neither team scored in the third or fourth innings, but with the Owls still leading 1-0, there was trouble on the horizon.

In the top of the fifth, L-Burg came out swinging, a couple of hard singles and a three-run homer by Tanner Goodsaint, the Lizards' clean-up hitter, cleared the bases. The Lizards led 3-1.

JJ got the next two Lizards out, but then the wheels fell off.

The tall right-hander walked three batters in a row, filling the bases. With each walk, the Lizards' fans got louder and louder, and the Owls' fans grew more worried. JJ and the Owls were in a jam, and everyone knew it.

As the batter jogged to first base, Jack anxiously chomped on his gum and fidgeted with his glove. He watched as JJ wiped the beads of sweat from his face and rolled his shoulder, trying to shake off the tension.

Coach Wolf knew it was time for a change. "Time!" he called out and slowly walked towards the mound, his shoes kicking up small clouds of dust. The coach gathered the infielders for a quick chat, then handed the baseball to Noah.

"You can get this guy," Coach Wolf said with certainty. "Remember the change-up. It's your secret weapon."

Noah nodded and slammed the baseball into his glove. His eyes narrowed as he focused on Cooper behind home plate.

The stands buzzed with excitement. Everyone was on their feet, waiting to see what would happen next. Noah was getting ready to face Mike Smith. The Lizards' first baseman had a powerful swing and a keen eye. The bases were loaded, and the Owls couldn't let the Lizards score again.

Noah finished his last warmup toss and took a deep breath. His fastball had plenty of zip, and his change-ups were perfect. Cooper fired the ball back to the lefthander, who confidently nodded, waiting for the Lizards' hitter to come to the plate.

An equally confident Mike marched to home plate, his eyes full of determination. The fearsome hitter smacked his bat on the plate before he shot Noah a fierce stare, daring him to throw a strike.

The umpire pointed to Noah, his voice cutting through the crowd noise. "Play ball!"

Noah got his sign and unleashed a fastball that zipped straight towards Cooper's open mitt. Mike took a huge swing, but he was late. Nothing but air…

"Strike one!" the umpire yelled as Cooper gave a nod and fired the ball back to the mound.

Undeterred, Mike dug back in, his gaze sharpening. Noah, feeling bold by the first pitch, threw another fastball. Mike swung hard, and smack! The ball shot off his bat, a rocket shot flying toward the left-field line. It curved foul, bouncing off the fence with a loud *clank*.

The crowd's energy surged, a mix of cheers and gasps filling the air. Everyone was on the edge of their seats. Activity at the concession stand stood still. All eyes were on the field. That powerful swing was nearly a disaster for the Owls.

"Whew, he ripped that fastball," Jack whispered, his eyes wide.

With the count 0-2, Noah looked at Coach Wolf, who gave a little nod. It was time for the secret weapon, the change-up. Noah nodded back. This was the right time. Noah took a deep breath, checked the runners, and let the ball fly.

Using the exact arm speed and grip Preston taught him, the pitch looked like a fastball. Mike's eyes got big as he swung way too early. The bat sliced through the air, hitting nothing but the afternoon breeze. It was the perfect pitch at the perfect time.

"Strike three!" the umpire boomed.

The L-burg fans couldn't believe it, sighing and shaking their heads. But the Owls' side erupted with shouting and clapping. "Way to go Noah!" rang out.

Jack sprinted to Noah, giving him the biggest high five. The rest of the team followed, patting Noah on the back and cheering. Noah, still smiling, spotted Preston walking out of the Lizards' dugout. Preston, lips pressed together, gave him a nod. Noah nodded right back.

The Owls zoomed into the dugout. Coach Wolf pointed to the Energy Meter. The arrow was maxed out in the green. Despite being down 3-1, the game was far from over.

"Let's get the bats going!" Coach Wolf encouraged. "You guys are good hitters. Take it one pitch at a time and do your routine. It's just you and the baseball up there. See the ball, hit the ball!"

Fired up, the Owls got to work. Jordan kicked off the rally with a solid single to left. The next two Owls reached base, with Drew getting a rare walk from Preston and Chase tapping an infield single. The bases were jam-packed with Owls. But Cooper struck out on a fastball for the first out.

Now, it was up to Matt, Oak Grove's best hitter. The Owls' slugger confidently made his way to home plate. The air buzzed with excitement. Both sides of the stands were the loudest they'd been all day. But the noise didn't faze him. Matt was all business. He loved being in a big spot like this.

Jack stood at the edge of the dugout and stared out at the field. With fingers crossed behind him, he whispered, "You got this, Matt. If anyone can do it, you can."

"He always looks confident," Danny said to Jack, almost yelling so he could be heard over the frenzied crowd.

Jack nodded, a small smile playing on his lips. "He's such a good hitter. I bet Preston throws him a change-up."

"No way, he's gonna get a fastball," Danny said and banged loudly on a metal trash can.

Preston wound up, his arm whirling like a tornado as he unleashed a fastball straight down the middle. Matt had been watching Preston all game, learning, and waiting for this moment. As the ball zoomed closer, time seemed to slow. Matt's guess was right, a fastball. The bat met the ball with a loud crack, soaring into the open sky and over the head of the left fielder.

"Go! Go! Go!" Coach Wolf yelled as he windmilled the runners around third base.

By the time the ball made it back to the infield, all three Owls crossed the plate, and Matt stood on second base. The Owls took the lead 4-3!

"I knew it!" Jack couldn't help but shout, his voice lost in the sea of cheers.

"Way to go, Matt!" he tried to yell across the field, but the crowd's roar swallowed his words whole.

Preston quickly settled down and struck out the next two Owls, stranding Matt on second, ending the inning. The game had changed, as the scoreboard showed the Owls in the lead, 4-3.

"Everyone, let's hustle out! Last inning!" Coach Wolf's voice echoed off the dugout walls, his hands clapping like thunderclaps. "Stay sharp and play good defense!" he shouted. The team sprang into action, dashing to their positions with renewed energy. The game hung in the balance.

Get three more outs and the game is ours, Jack thought as he tossed a perfect throw to first base.

As Noah warmed up, Jack saw the lefty was getting tired. His fastball had lost its zip. The Lizards had adjusted to Noah's once-unstoppable changeup. Jack knew that getting these last three outs wouldn't be easy.

As the first Lizard came to bat, Jack hollered encouragement, "C'mon, Noah! You've got this!" His glove smacked against his thigh, sending up a small cloud of dust.

Noah's first pitch was smashed but right at Danny, the shortstop, who caught it on a line.

"Great job, Danny!" Jack said. He held a finger in the air. "One down!"

Whew, that was ripped. He's got nothing left. I hope Noah can finish this game, Jack thought, trying not to look worried.

On the very next pitch, Chase had to sprint to the fence in right field to catch a long fly. Noah's not-so-tricky change-up almost ended up going out of the park. Two down, bases empty.

"That was close!" Jack said with a sigh of relief. *One more out. Just one more out,* he thought.

The Lizards weren't giving up. Sharp back-to-back singles by Jaiden and Hendrix, put the tying run on second and the game in doubt. Everyone could tell that Noah's arm was worn out. Somehow, the Owls needed to get just one more out.

Next up was Tanner, the Lizards' dangerous hitter who homered the last time up. Noah knew he had to be really careful in this spot. He was careful, alright, too careful, as he walked Tanner on four pitches. The bases were now full of Lizards. Their fans were screaming with excitement. Coach Wolf called a timeout and headed to the mound. Jack and the rest of the infielders joined him.

The bases were loaded, and the Oak Grove Owls clung to the slimmest of leads, 4-3. Everyone was on the edge of their seats, eyes glued to the mound, wondering what the coach would do.

Coach Wolf rubbed the side of his face. "Noah, I'm going to make a change here." The coach's eyes settled on Jack. "The mound's yours, Jack. Get us an out."

"You got it," Jack said, nodding firmly. He hadn't pitched much this year, but knew this was his chance to prove himself. His heart pounded with excitement. As he warmed up, his pitches flew in every direction except where he wanted them to go.

Take a few deep breaths. Just slow down, Jack thought.

The Lizards' batter was none other than Alex, Jack's best friend. They'd never faced each other. Jack felt a storm of feelings inside him—eager to pitch against Alex, but anxious about what could happen. Jack took a moment and walked behind the mound, wiping his sweaty forehead.

Alex is tough, but I can get him. Calm down. Take a few breaths, he thought as he scratched the dirt with his cleat. Jack got back on the mound and looked at his catcher.

Alex stepped into the batter's box, a serious look etched on his face. Jack wound up and threw as hard as he could, but his fastball was way too high.

"Ball one!" the umpire shouted.

Jack's heart sank a little. He shook his head and took a deep breath, trying to calm down.

Jack's next pitch was way outside, and Cooper made a diving save to prevent a game-tying wild pitch.

"Ball two!" The umpire called out.

Jack's shoulders tightened. He felt a knot forming in his stomach. "Gotta throw a strike," he muttered to himself. His mind is going a mile a minute. But his next pitch also missed the mark.

"Ball three," the umpire shouted. The Owls' crowd groaned.

Jack felt another sudden wave of panic. *Another ball and the game is tied. Don't walk him,* he thought as he took off his hat and ran the back of his hand across his forehead. *I can't mess this up. I just can't.*

Standing behind the mound, Jack felt the pressure crushing down on him. The more he thought about messing up, the more his heart pounded. His worry and doubt haunted him.

What if I blow this? I can't walk him.

An image of the umpire calling ball four flashed in his head.

Just then, a loud voice from center field interrupted his thoughts. "Reset, Jack! Reset! One pitch at a time! Take it pitch by pitch!" Matt yelled above the crowd. "You can do it!"

Hearing Matt, Jack remembered the lessons about positive self-talk. "Say what you *want* to have happen, not what you are *afraid of,*" Jack whispered. He took a deep breath and let the advice sink in. "Hit your spot," he told himself firmly. Gone were the images of ball four, replaced by the sight of his pitch smacking into Cooper's waiting mitt.

Jack stepped back onto the mound and stood tall, staring at his catcher's target. This pitch was the only thing that mattered. One pitch at a time.

Hit your spot, he repeated silently.

With eyes narrowed, Jack let the ball fly. The pitch was perfect, right towards Copper's mitt. Alex let it go by.

Strike one!

The crowd erupted in cheers, and Jack felt a spark of hope. His confidence boosted by the last pitch, Jack kept the positive self-talk going. Again, he threw a pitch, right where he wanted it. Alex swung and missed.

Strike two!

The game was hanging by a thread, and Jack's newfound confidence was shining through. With the count now at 3-2, the next pitch could decide everything. Jack gave a long look into Cooper. Even though the crowd noise was at a fever's pitch, Jack couldn't hear anything. It was complete concentration.

Jack got his sign. Cooper wanted a 3-2 fastball. Jack took a breath and sent the ball spinning towards Alex. It was going to be strike three, but Alex swung.

Crack!

The baseball jumped off the bat. It was a line drive to center field, racing towards the ground. The Lizard runners dashed from their bases, kicking up infield dust. Jack turned and watched the speeding ball, his eyes wide and heart pounding. A hush fell over the crowd.

With his eyes locked on the ball, Matt sprinted forward, determined to make the catch. In a split-second decision, he flung himself into the air, his glove extended in a daring dive. Everyone froze, holding their breath as Matt hit the ground, the dust swirling around him. Then he got up, holding his glove up high. And there it was: the ball! He caught it!

"Out!" the umpire shouted.

Game over! The Owls won!

The Owls swarmed Matt before turning to Jack. A whirlwind of high fives and cheers celebrated their big win. Jack realized something important. It wasn't just his arm that won the game; it was his mental game. By changing his thoughts, he changed the game.

The Owls and the Lizards shook hands and as the teams started clearing the field, Jack and Alex lingered at home plate.

"That last at-bat of yours was pretty intense," Jack said, giving Alex a friendly nudge.

Alex chuckled. "Yeah, but watch out! Next time I'm coming for you."

Jack's smile widened. "Guess we'll see about that!"

Jack's tone became a bit more serious. "Hey, thanks for having your dad teach us about the mental game. It really changed how we play."

Alex's head bobbed in agreement. "It showed. We got the lead, and you guys kept fighting. You played like a different team. The mental game stuff really works, huh?"

"It sure does," Jack agreed, feeling a sense of pride for his team.

Jack noticed Noah and Preston chatting and laughing. It was as if they had been friends for years, not rivals on opposing teams. Jack couldn't help but smile at Noah's new attitude towards his longtime friends, the Lizards. Noah looked at Jack; the two caught gazes and nodded.

Just then, Coaches Wolf and Ranger called the boys together in the outfield. They stood side by side. The players huddled around, all eyes glued on the coaches.

Coach Ranger started, "I just want to say how proud I am of all of you. You really showed us what it means to play hard and respect the game of baseball and each other. Seeing you all shake hands and share laughs after the game, that's what sports are about. Play hard and compete, but show great sportsmanship, win or lose! Great job!"

Coach Wolf chimed in, "What also caught my eye was how well both teams used their mental game skills. Your deep breathing, your routines before each pitch, and how you focused on winning the next pitch—that all made a difference. Keep practicing those skills. They're valuable life skills and can help you off the field, too."

For the Owls and Lizards, the game of baseball brought them together, teaching them lessons that went far beyond today's game. For Jack, today wasn't just about winning or losing; it was about growing and learning. He knew these were the moments he would remember—the moments that made the game of baseball truly great.

You're Up to Bat!

Jack says it's your turn to shine! Answering the questions helps you score runs. Answer one question? That's a single. Two? You've got a double. Three gets you a triple; four is a home run, and all five? You've hit a grand slam! Let's swing for the fences!

Chapters 9 & 10

1. What advice did Jack give Noah before he batted against Preston? Did it work?

2. What were the mental game skills Jack used during the game?

3. What mental game skill did Preston use after a tough moment?

4. The coaches liked how both teams showed good sportsmanship. Find examples of good sportsmanship in the chapter.

5. What did you like best about the story? Share what you learned with a friend, teammate, parent, or your coach!

Coaches' Guide

Pitch by Pitch!

Chapter 1- Practice, Pressure, and Ice Cream

We meet Jack and his baseball team, the Oak Grove Owls. They're eager but nervous about their upcoming tournament. The Owls' first game is against their archrivals, the Lattasburg Lizards. The twist? Jack played for the Lizards. The chapter introduces the importance of mental game skills, while also exploring themes of friendship, rivalry, and sportsmanship.

Team Activities - Chapter 1

1. Tell your players to share a story about a time they played a game against a friend. Ask them how they felt.

2. Talk about what being a good sport means. Ask the team to share examples of good and bad sportsmanship they've seen. Discuss your team's sportsmanship standards and expectations.

3. Ask your team what they think 'the mental game' means. See what they already know about the mental game.

Chapter 2 - Storm Clouds Over the Diamond

Jack faces a mix of emotions as he prepares to compete against his former teammates, the Lizards. Some Owls, including Noah, question his loyalty. How will he handle his close friendships with players from his old team and Noah's attitude? The showdown between the Owls and Lizards does not go well. The Owls play terribly, with physical mistakes and a poor mental game. Jack has a reflective moment at the end of a tough day.

Team Activities - Chapter 2

1. Ask, "What do you think makes a great teammate?" Get everyone's ideas.

2. Ask, "What made Coach Wolf unhappy about the Owls' game against the Lizards?"

3. Ask, "How do you feel when you win or lose?" Talk about the best ways to deal with both.

Chapter 3 - The Owls' Game Plan: Win One Pitch at a Time

A surprise visitor shows up at the Owls' practice: the Lizards' coach. Coach Ranger, a former pro player and coach, helps them kick-start their journey to master mental game skills. Their first lesson: play one pitch at a time. The Owls learn that the foundation of playing outstanding baseball involves focusing on winning the most important pitch in any game: the very next one.

Team Activities - Chapter 3

1. Ask, "What's the main goal of every player in every game?" Hint: It's about focusing on the next pitch.

2. Say, "Let's think about focusing on one pitch at a time. What can distract you from staying focused on that next pitch?"

3. Create 'Win the Next Pitch' reminders, such as posters or bag tags, to emphasize the importance of focusing on one pitch at a time. (Luggage tags from the dollar store are great to use.)

Chapter 4 – The First Three Puzzle Pieces

Coach Ranger teaches the Owls the first three pieces of the mental game puzzle. He stresses the importance of learning something new every day, playing with high energy, and always having an Arrows-Out attitude. The boys learn how to apply these skills on the field and in their everyday lives. Coach also introduces them to some awesome mental game tools like personal learning notebooks and the Energy Meter.

Team Activities - Chapter 4

1. Remind players it's important to learn something new every day, just like the pros do. Ask, "What are some things you learned at our last practice or our last game?"

2. Create your own learning notebook for each player and coach. Players write down things they learn about baseball and themselves. Review the notebooks, either individually or in the group, regularly! (Small notebooks can also be purchased at the dollar store and then personalized.)

3. Create a cool Energy Meter for your team and post it in the dugout.

4. Ask each player to share examples of what Arrows-In and Arrows-Out players look like during a game.

5. Make Arrows-Out posters for the dugout, laminate them, and switch them up for each game. You can do this with any of the mental game lessons, such as 'Win the Next Pitch,' the '3 Ts,' etc.

Chapter 5 – Training Your Brain Like a Puppy

Focus is the key puzzle piece. Coach Ranger teaches the team they can choose which thoughts to focus on during a game. Distractions like the weather, mistakes, or worrying about the other team can pull their focus away. The Owls learn to focus on what they can control, like attitude and effort. The team then learns a simple method to regain focus during a game: notice when you're getting distracted, tell yourself 'STOP,' and use your own refocus phrase to return to the next pitch.

Team Activities - Chapter 5

1. Ask, "What does it feel like to be fully focused during a game?"

2. Talk about what things can distract them during a game and if they can control these distractions.

3. Remind players to only worry about things they can control, like effort and energy, not things they can't.

4. Ask the team what three steps they can take to quickly get focused again if distracted.

5. Get everyone to share their special phrase that helps them refocus.

Chapter 6 - Strike Out Doubt: Self-Talk Secrets

The team learns about the power of positive self-talk. Coach Ranger teaches the boys four proven self-talk tips. These tips help players stay calm under pressure and boost their confidence. The Owls also learn how they can use these self-talk tips, anywhere and anytime. Positive self-talk is important when playing baseball but also when dealing with life's challenges.

Team Activities - Chapter 6

1. Ask, "What is self-talk, and why do you think it's important?"

2. Ask for examples of negative and positive self-talk they've used or heard before.

3. Talk about how positive self-talk isn't just for sports. Where else could it help?

4. Review the four self-talk tips and talk about how your team can use them during their next game.

5. Have players pair up, with one player making a negative self-talk statement and the other player changing it to positive self-talk. Switch roles.

Chapter 7 - Controlling Emotions: Resetting with the 3 Ts

The Owls learn how to bounce back quickly if things go wrong during a game. Coach Ranger shows them how to deal with anxiety, frustration, and anger by doing things like deep breathing and using the '3 Ts.' This helps players focus on what's most important: the next pitch. Through interactive exercises and team discussions, the players discover how to use these strategies to control their emotions on and off the field.

Team Activities - Chapter 7

1. Ask how players feel after making a mistake and what usually happens if they can't shake it off.

2. Talk about why having a 'reset button' can help players forget mistakes and focus on the next pitch.

3. Practice deep breathing as a team. Make sure everyone is doing it correctly.

4. Ask about the 3 Ts of resetting and have players show how they'll use the 3 Ts in a game. Coaches, remind your players to use the 3 Ts when they make a mistake in practice. Players need these steps to become automatic during games.

5. Let players draw a comic strip of a baseball player using the 3 Ts to bounce back from a mistake.

Chapter 8 - Pre-Pitch Routines: Stop Thinking and Start Hitting!

The final piece of the Owls' mental game puzzle is pre-pitch routines, which are crucial for hitting, pitching, or fielding. This chapter teaches a scientific method to replace the superstitious pre-pitch routines many young players use. The team learns and practices a quality pre-pitch routine. The Owls are amazed at the results.

Team Activities - Chapter 8

1. Discuss why pre-pitch routines are helpful.

2. Have players imagine they're walking to home plate. What are the four steps of their routine?

3. Talk to each player about their focus point. Make sure it's something on the bat that's small and unique.

4. Practice pre-pitch routines in the batting cage. Make sure they take their time to get it right. Too often, players want to hurry through it, especially the focus point. You want your players to look at the focus point until there are zero thoughts, even if it takes a few extra seconds. The goal during initial training is to make sure they experience what it's like to hit without thinking. We want to train complete external narrow focus on the baseball coming from the release point and reacting to it. Don't rush the routine when they're first learning. The pre-pitch routine gets quicker with practice.

5. In batting practice and before games, have players do their routine like it's a real game. Rehearsing this, even a few times,

pays off later. This type of practice can be done with simple front toss.

Chapters 9 & 10 - It's the Owls vs. the Lizards: The Rematch of the Year! / Trouble for the Owls?

The Oak Grove Owls face off against their rivals, the Lattasburg Lizards, in a tense game. Will Jack and the Owls finally overcome the Lizards, or will Oak Grove face another defeat? As the game unfolds, Jack and his teammates put their new mental game skills into practice. Along the way, both teams discover important lessons in sportsmanship, teamwork, and the value of using their mental game skills.

Team Activities - Chapter 9 & 10

1. Have players list the seven mental game skills the Owls learned. Ask them which skills they find most helpful.

2. Talk about how the Owls used their new mental skills in the second game against the Lizards.

3. Make a poster of these skills and put it up in the dugout.

4. Ask the players to share the sportsmanship moments from that game.

5. Talk to every player one-on-one about their mental game skills. See which skills they're confident in and which ones need extra practice.

Coaches, keep working on these mental game skills all season. They're just as important as physical skills. Consistent practice is the key to success!

Acknowledgments

As this book finds its way into the world, it's important to take a moment and acknowledge those who have made these pages possible. A book is not created by one person alone, but by a harmonious blend of minds, voices, and encouragement. I want to express my deepest gratitude to the amazing team of editors and illustrators who have brought this story to life.

Olivia Fischer deserves the first note of thanks for her discerning eye and exceptional editing. Your edits not only polished the manuscript but also ensured that it spoke with clarity and impact. Thank you for your help with this project and for always pushing me to improve as a writer.

My wife, Dianne, thank you for supporting me through the ups and downs of this creative project. Your ability to be patient, encouraging, and offer insightful feedback has been a source of comfort and inspiration. Your careful proofreading, thought-provoking plot twist discussions, and remarkable ability to grasp my convoluted ideas have enhanced both the book and my growth as a writer. I am very grateful for your help in making this book a reality.

To the thousands of readers who have followed my work through the years, your support has been the foundation upon which my dreams have been built. Your excitement and admiration for my previous books have fueled my determination to take on this new project. As a self-published author, the significance of your willingness to share and recommend my books cannot be overstated. I am deeply thankful for each and every one of you.

With sincere appreciation,

Curt

Author's Note

As we turn the final pages of "Pitch by Pitch! Winning Mental Game Strategies for Young Baseball Players," I truly hope you and your son enjoyed every bit of it, finding it more than just a good read, but a real game-changer in your baseball adventures.

This book comes from a place of deep personal significance. I know how tough baseball can be, especially the mental game. I vividly recall the struggles of my youth on the baseball diamond. Despite the hours of practice and my deep passion for the game, I would get nervous, lose confidence, and not play as well as I knew I could. In those days, the concept of mental coaching in sports was virtually non-existent. There were no sports psychologists to consult or relevant books to guide us through those tough games. We were left to our own devices, trying to solve problems we barely understood.

Including the Lattasburg Lizards is a nod to my own roots, a reminder of where my love for baseball began. Some of the happiest moments of my life were spent growing up in Lattasburg, playing ball with my brothers and friends, nearly 50 years ago. I didn't just learn about sports; I also learned about friendship, determination, and having fun, no matter what.

It is my hope that "Pitch by Pitch!" serves not just as a manual for mental game strategies, but also as a reminder of the joy and passion that baseball can bring into our lives. If this book has touched you or your son's journey in baseball, I encourage you to share its message with friends, family, and fellow coaches.

Until we meet again in the pages of my next adventure, keep striving for excellence, not just on the field, but in every aspect of your life.

Warmest regards,

Curt

About the Author

Dr. Curt Ickes, a licensed clinical psychologist specializing in sport psychology, harbors a profound passion for baseball. His interest in merging psychological principles with athletic performance has been the cornerstone of his career. With over 30 years of experience teaching psychology, Dr. Ickes now holds the title of Emeritus Faculty at Ashland University and continues to contribute to the AU baseball team's success. Beyond his commitment to the Eagles, he collaborates with numerous baseball and softball teams and has notably served as the sport psychologist for the professional baseball team, the Lake Erie Crushers.

Dr. Ickes has authored best-selling titles, including *Win the Next Pitch!* and *You Got This!,* which introduce young baseball and softball players (ages 8-12) to important mental game strategies. *Mental Toughness: Getting the Edge*, his first publication, caters to high school and college players seeking to learn more advanced mental game skills. These works are available on Amazon.com.

Curt's books not only deepen young athletes' appreciation for baseball but also teach effective mental game strategies that elevate their performance. These mental game skills extend far beyond the baseball field. They nurture self-esteem, encourage effective teamwork, and equip young athletes with the tools to manage the emotional rollercoaster associated with life's wins and losses.

Made in the USA
Las Vegas, NV
19 June 2024

91220123R00085